Praise for
PRAYING THROUGH INFERTILITY

"Infertility can be a lonely and isolating experience. In her devotional, *Praying Through Infertility*, Jennifer Crowley breaks through that loneliness to identify the complex emotions associated with this experience, as well as the impact it has on personal identity, marriages, and one's relationship with God. By sharing her personal story and connecting it to the litany she prayerfully composed, Jennifer acknowledges the uniqueness of every person's experience, while forging a connection among all who carry this cross by naming the emotions and situations so many of us find in common. This devotional truly is a place of spiritual respite and comfort."

—Ann M. Koshute, MTS, Co-Founder
Springs in the Desert, Catholic Infertility Ministry

"In *Praying Through Infertility*, Jen prayerfully walks with the reader day by day through an entire cycle, echoing the cries of her heart and helping to restore hope in her future. This devotional is creative, unique, and feels like a friend holding one hand and the other placed in the hand of Jesus. This book will truly be a blessing to each reader!"

—Mary Bruno, author of *Twelve Stripes Deep*,
co-founder of *fabmbase.org*

"I wish I'd held this devotional when I was struggling with infertility. Jen offers a litany of prayers that are so relatable and valuable, one that I haven't encountered before. She gives practical tips using Bible verses and reflection guides that would be perfect for individual retreats or support groups that moves people toward healing. This is a great addition to the few Catholic resources for those carrying the cross of infertility and ministries supporting them. Thanks, Jen, for sharing your story and the fruit of your sufferings."

—Janelle C. Florendo, Certified FertilityCare Practitioner
NFP Coordinator and Responsible Practitioner, FertilityCare Services: Diocese of Charleston, SC

"If you're a woman who has experienced infertility, you'll find solace and affirmation in the pages of Jen's new devotional. Jen bravely put into words many thoughts and emotions I've experienced but stuffed down because of shame. I was relieved to find I'm not the only one who has had these 'crazy' thoughts while riding the roller coaster that is infertility.

"Along with companionship, you'll find challenge on these pages. The Bible and all the stories of barren women being blessed with a child (or children) after years of persistent prayer have become triggers for me. Jen pulls out lines of Scripture that provide comfort and strength as we carry this cross on our life's journey.
It was an affirming and healing read."

—KATHRYN WOOD, M.ED., author of *Waiting with Mary: A Seven Sorrows Devotional for Catholic Women Facing Infertility*

Praying Through Infertility
A litany and devotional for women

Volume One:
The Stormy Waves of Grief

Praying Through Infertility

A litany and devotional for women

Volume One:
The Stormy Waves of Grief

Jennifer Crowley

Copyright © 2025 by Jennifer Crowley
All rights reserved.
Printed in the United States of America

ISBN # 979-8-9892839-0-3

Published by Journey of Faith Publishing, LLC
Austin, Texas

Names: Crowley, Jennifer, author.
Title: Praying Through Infertility: a litany and devotional for women, Volume One: The Stormy Waves of Grief / Jennifer Crowley.

Scripture quotes are taken from the New American Bible, Revised Edition. Copyright © 2011 by Confraternity of Christian Doctrine, all rights reserved.

Cover image © istockphoto.com/Milatoo

It is the Publisher's goal to minimize disruption caused by technical errors or invalid websites. While all links are active at the time of publication, because of the dynamic nature of the internet, some web addresses or links contained in this book may have changed and may no longer be valid. Journey of Faith Publishing bears no responsibility for the continuity or content of the external sites, nor for that of subsequent links. Contact the external site for answers regarding its content.

To my husband, Mark,
who's shared the cross of infertility with me,
for being an incredible, strong and supportive companion
with whom to share my life's journey.

To the men and women with whom I've been privileged to walk
through the ministry of Sarah's Hope & Abraham's Promise.
Your witness of steadfast faith through times of trial
as well as your courage and support have been nothing
less than inspirational. I wouldn't have survived my own
infertility journey without the gift of your presence and
willingness to be vulnerable.

JENNIFER CROWLEY

ACKNOWLEDGMENTS

This book project has taken many years to come to fruition. Thank you to all who have encouraged me and prayed for this book from when I first put pen to paper to write it.

My parents and in-laws, Janice Jones, Dennis and Debbie Jones, Judy and Rich Crowley.

My sister, Allison Merchant, and my best friend, Angela Wilson, for allowing me to bare my soul endless times and for your tireless support, encouragement and listening ears.

Cari Henry, MD, for helping to create a place for me, and so many others, to learn how to grow in holiness through the struggle of infertility, how to live through it with increased faith and hope, no matter what life brings, and for giving me the opportunity to minister to others going through similar experiences.

My sister-in-law, Veronica Crowley, for design and production coordination.

CONTENTS

Author's Note xiii
Foreword by Lauren Allen xvii
Introduction xxi
Litany for Women Struggling With Infertility 1

    Week 1 | Prayers Seeking Freedom from Waves of Hopelessness 8

    Week 2 | Prayers Seeking Freedom from Waves of Egotism 30

    Week 3 | Prayers Seeking Freedom from Waves of Contempt 55

    Week 4 | Prayers Seeking Freedom from Waves of Anger 74

    Week 5 | Prayers Seeking Freedom from Waves of Despising God 99

Closing Prayer of Discernment 125
Final Thoughts 128
Appendix: Additional Resources 130
Examination of Conscience for Those Suffering from Infertility 138
About the Author 147

AUTHOR'S NOTE

The Stormy Waves of Grief

Then He made the disciples get into the boat and precede Him to the other side, while He dismissed the crowds. After doing so, He went up on the mountain by Himself to pray. When it was evening He was there alone. Meanwhile the boat, already a few miles offshore, was being tossed about by the waves, for the wind was against it. During the fourth watch of the night, He came toward them, walking on the sea. When the disciples saw Him walking on the sea they were terrified. "It is a ghost," they said, and they cried out in fear. At once [Jesus] spoke to them, "Take courage, it is I; do not be afraid."

Peter said to Him in reply, "Lord, if it is you, command me to come to you on the water." He said, "Come." Peter got out of the boat and began to walk on the water toward Jesus. But when he saw how [strong] the wind was he became frightened; and, beginning to sink, he cried out, "Lord, save me!" Immediately Jesus stretched out His hand and caught him, and said to him, "O you of little faith, why did you doubt?" After they got into the boat, the wind died down. Those who were in the boat did Him homage, saying, "Truly, you are the Son of God."

—Matthew 14:22-33

"The Walking on the Water" is one of my favorite passages in the Bible. Peter, who represents any one of us, longs to do the impossible—walk on the water to meet Jesus. The story moves me because I can so clearly see myself in the restless sea, the difficulties leading to momentary weakness, even crises of faith. I can hear Jesus speak to me, asking, "O you of little faith, why did you doubt?"

St. Matthew's retelling is full of hope, expectation, courage, fear, anxiety, desperation, uncertainty and awe—the same emotions we experience in our infertility journeys. And just like Peter, who is at one moment full of faith and then completely void of it in another, the journey of infertility parallels this rollercoaster of emotions and inner conflict.

It's not hard to feel like we, too, are in that boat, being tossed about by the waves and the wind every time we muster up the courage to hope to conceive. When we adhere to a rigid medication schedule, doctor and lab appointments and obsessively examine our body's fertility signs in order to calculate the perfect days to engage in the marital act. When we then endure two weeks of agony to see if our efforts proved successful. When we're asked—for what seems like the hundredth time—when we're going to have kids. When we find ourselves sitting through yet another pregnancy announcement, all while trying to remain positive and have trust in God. When we learn with the beginning of menstruation that another cycle has passed without conception. When we repeat these stages of grief every month and are exhausted.

Given how these constant ups and downs of infertility mimic the rough waters of a stormy sea and our experiences parallel Peter's, I decided to subtitle this devotional for women suffering through infertility, "The Stormy Waves of Grief." The prayers offered in this volume—the first of three—are meant to uncover within us and name out loud all of the big, and sometimes tumultuous, emotions and feelings we experience when we first begin to think about "infertility." My hope with this devotional is to validate each and every emotion, struggle and temptation that, undoubtedly, arises at some point in our family building journeys.

As you go through this book, I ask you to picture yourself in the boat as it's being tossed about by turbulent winds and to be intentional about visualizing who is with you. You are not alone. I'm in the boat with you, along with every woman who has found herself suffering through the raw, overwhelming reality of infertility.

Most importantly, Jesus is waiting to catch you with open arms.

In solidarity and with courage, let's face the storm together and see where God is asking us to go in this journey.

FOREWORD

Infertility is such a heavy cross to carry. It's often a cross that we pray we can throw away. *Lord, if I can just get pregnant… this will all be over. Please Lord, heal me. I will raise my children to know, serve and love you!* That was my prayer in January of 2021. I was not expecting to receive a vivid, instantaneous response (how often does that happen in prayer?), but to my surprise I got one that has forever changed the projection of my life. I heard so clearly: "Your cross is meant to be carried." It was exactly the scolding that I needed. Our cross may be a heavy one to carry, but it does serve a purpose. It is meant to serve a purpose. I needed to stop praying for my cross to disappear, and instead I needed to dive into what the weight meant. I desperately needed to dive into prayer and listen to what was being asked of me.

I will never forget that moment, because that angry conversation with God brought on the creation of the International Catholic Infertility Ministry, The Fruitful Hollow. I've often told people that I don't know how this ministry came to fruition because I did very little. That probably sounds foolish coming from the founder and director. The Holy Spirit worked at a level that I had not seen before; everything came together almost instantaneously. Within a few weeks, we had an international team of women. I had no prior knowledge of any of these women before that moment. The Holy Spirit brought us a professional editor, theological editor, resource manager, lead for our mentorship ministry and so many other incredible writers, mentors and prayer warriors. Three years later, these women have become some of my closest friends; they are more like family. I will forever be truly humbled by the power of God. He has redeemed the weight of my cross by allowing me to accompany others. Even in the darkest of situations, He has shown me that He is constant. He is there. He is with you in every breath. Every moment. Yes, even now.

If at this moment you're struggling carrying or trying to figure out how to carry your cross, I implore you to consider the following questions: What might God have in store for you that would redeem all of the pain from this cross? Why was this cross meant to be carried? Why is this cross *your* cross? This cross was meant to be *your* cross.

I have good news for those of you who are having a visceral reaction to the statement above; nothing says we have to carry it alone. Even Jesus did not carry His cross alone. On His way to Calvary, Christ was sent Simon, a Cyrenian, to help Him on His way. "As they led him away they took hold of a certain Simon, a Cyrenian, who was coming in from the country; and after laying the cross on him, they made him carry it behind Jesus" (Lk 23:26).

When I first read through *Praying Through Infertility*, I was struck by the depth and magnitude of support it offers. For the times when you desperately need prayer but don't have the words, this is your Simon. For the times when you're working through the muck you've picked up on the way, use this as your aid. Personally, reading this book for the first time was like looking into a mirror that held my deepest truths. All of the hurt, guilt, frustration and anger that I held shut up into the deepest parts of my soul were brought swiftly to the surface. Here I was, and here they were. We were in a staredown. Even though facing these dark wounds was an ugly process, we did meet in the most amazing place; because of this book, we met in prayer.

When Jen reached out to me and asked if I would mind writing this foreword, I hesitated because I did not want to commit to writing a foreword for a resource that I did not find helpful. However, when I received the manuscript, I could not call her back fast enough. It was instantly clear to me how instrumental this book will become and how desperately this resource is needed. This is not a book written by someone who "sort of gets it." The pages of this book are written from the wood of Jen's personal cross. A cross that is just as heavy as yours is. The prayers that are within this book are raw, honest and piercing. This book will take you deeper than expected into wounds you didn't realize you had. All for the healing and redemption of the weight of this cross.

Jen and I have talked about how when you face your cross head-on, redemption does happen. Fruitfulness happens. I have no doubt that this book will lead to an abundance of fruit in the prayer life of the infertility community. To face your cross head-on is no easy task, but this book is a truly exceptional guide. As we know, there is no instruction book for infertility. But because Jen listened to the Holy Spirit, we now have a guide to accompany us in a practical way. It is my prayer that this book will meet you when you need it most. May it lead you closer to Christ; He redeems all things.

Lauren Allen
Director & Founder
The Fruitful Hollow

INTRODUCTION

To say that living with infertility is hard is a gross understatement.

The rollercoaster of emotions and physical demands infertility brings will pull you in ways you've never known. Having issues with such a natural part of life, one you always assumed you would experience as a woman, can take your breath away. It's certainly a most unwelcome surprise that knocks you right off your feet.

Being unable to conceive or carry a child is such an intimate and personal struggle that it's hard to know who to turn to for support. Sharing your story can involve discussing your body and marriage in ways you never thought you would with anyone other than your spouse. At the same time, though, the sorrow you carry feels too heavy to bear alone.

Infertility affects you physically, emotionally, mentally, financially and spiritually. It brings unrest and strife to marriages, with some ending tragically.

...the sorrow you carry feels too heavy to bear alone.

It strains your extended family and other relationships. People who haven't experienced infertility have a hard time understanding your sorrow and heartache. They don't always say the right things, or anything at all when you need them to. They may not know what you're going through because you're suffering in silence. So, you withdraw from them even more because their innocent lack of sensitivity to your family building frustrates you.

It impacts your job performance. Racing thoughts often consume you, and you get distracted or become increasingly unmotivated to carry out daily responsibilities.

On top of these hardships, many who struggle with infertility experience a crisis of faith. God tells us, *"Be fruitful and multiply" (Gn 1:28a).* But you wonder, if God wants you to heed His words, why are you and your spouse unable to conceive? Confusion and anger cause you to question God and your faith—adding guilt to all that you're feeling.

The Church is seriously lacking in Her ministry to couples struggling with infertility, too. Granted, the Church is stretched thin and has a lot on Her plate—but still. Being unable to find spiritual support during such an overwhelming time of life leaves too many to suffer alone.

There's no denying the pain and grief that often come with this seemingly unbearable cross at times. Living with infertility is hard.

My Infertility Story

My husband, Mark, and I have struggled with infertility for more than a decade.

For the first year of our marriage, we chose to avoid pregnancy using Natural Family Planning. As part of our marriage preparation, we had taken fertility awareness classes to learn the Sympto-Thermal Method and become informed of my body's windows of fertility and infertility. We spent that first year of marriage learning how to live together as husband and wife, wanting to enjoy each other as a couple before growing our family. We vacationed in Cancun for our first married Thanksgiving and spent time setting up our first home—decorating, landscaping and creating our dream to-do list. We celebrated our first wedding anniversary with a two-week European vacation, living it up, because we knew we were both ready to start growing our family when we returned home. I remember being so excited and nervous at the same time.

Unbeknownst to us, I was already at the end of my peak fertility range when we married. We later learned that the ideal window for a woman to get pregnant, in terms of reproductive health, is between ages 17 to 28. I was 28.

The first month of our being open to conceiving came and went without a positive pregnancy test, but we weren't concerned about our fertility at that point. It isn't uncommon to not conceive on your first try. *We'll just try again next month*, I thought.

After three more months went by, however, and given my family history of severe endometriosis, my husband and I decided to make an appointment with a NaProTECHNOLOGY[1] doctor whom our hometown is blessed to have practicing. We discovered that I did indeed have severe endometriosis along with significant hormonal imbalances, ovulatory dysfunction and a uterine anomaly. All were affecting my fertility, so we started treatment immediately. Thus began our infertility journey.

Years passed, and I eventually found myself under the care of four fertility doctors in three cities in two states. Unbearably painful menstrual cramps from my endometriosis sent me to the emergency room some months. I underwent surgery five times to remove ever-returning endometriosis and to adjust the shape of my uterus to allow for a successful pregnancy. I can't even recall at this point exactly how many different medications I tried to help restore my fertility. Their laundry lists of daunting side effects influenced my mental, emotional and physical well-being, which didn't go unnoticed by my husband and close loved ones. For years, I went to a local radiology center four to five days in a row every month for ultrasounds to monitor ovulation. At our doctors'

---

[1] NaProTECHNOLOGY (Natural Procreative Technology) is a women's health science that monitors and maintains a woman's reproductive and gynecological health. It provides medical and surgical treatments that cooperate completely with the reproductive system. Learn more at *www.naprotechnology.com*.

recommendation, my husband and I learned a second method of fertility tracking, called the Creighton Model, because it reveals when couples are naturally fertile and infertile as well as abnormalities in a woman's health. With each month's passing, and the ending of one menstrual cycle into a new one, I moved from feelings of increasing hope and positivity to eventual disappointment and sorrow. Even with all of our efforts and multiple treatments, we've never been able to conceive.

Not long into our infertility journey, anguish, frustration and other feelings began weighing heavily on me. Not only did I feel that my roles as a woman and a wife were being challenged, but I also grappled with the spiritual component of being unable to conceive. I prayed fervently for physical healing and for the gift of a child, but month after month remained the same—with no baby. As others around me continued to get pregnant, I found myself being tempted to envy and withdrew from prayer. I grew increasingly disheartened with God's apparent silence and knew receiving some spiritual guidance might help. But my spiritual director had been transferred to a distant parish, and I couldn't find any ministries nearby that addressed what I was experiencing. Parish priests are rarely able to accommodate ongoing individual pastoral counseling. The secular support groups through the mainstream fertility center in town ignored the spiritual aspect of infertility.

While searching fruitlessly for the spiritual support I so desperately needed, I realized that something had to be done for couples like us who were suffering in isolation. I began talking to a friend, who had been a family medicine doctor and was familiar with the Church teaching on reproductive technology, about developing our own spiritual support ministry for those suffering from infertility. Together, we founded Sarah's Hope & Abraham's Promise, which we would later expand to serve couples suffering from pregnancy loss and early infant loss as well as those touched by adoption.

INTRODUCTION

Writing My Litany

One afternoon, an incident at work triggered a moment of anxiety regarding my infertility. I decided to start writing down all of my struggles with what had become a huge cross for me to bear.

I've always loved litanies and praying their responsive petitions between a leader and a group. But I couldn't find any litanies that relayed how I was feeling. As I wrote the struggles I was having as prayers, asking for God's help to overcome them, my infertility litany began to take shape. Each time an issue triggered a feeling, I incorporated it into the litany and turned that trigger into a prayer.

> *As I wrote the struggles I was having as prayers, asking for God's help to overcome them, my infertility litany began to take shape.*

As our infertility story continued to unfold, I learned about others with similar struggles. This led me to include specific prayers in my litany that might speak to those having the same temptations.

During the process of writing my litany, my eyes were finally opened to the blessings God has given me and my husband through our infertility struggle, and I was moved to add prayers of thanksgiving. When I felt the litany was complete, I also added lines asking for prayers of intercession from our patron saints along with other saints associated with infertility and desperate causes.

This devotional features my entire litany and guidance for praying through a third of it in five weeks. Including reflections and prayers over each line would've made for one very long devotional, so I decided to break up what I wrote into thirds. Two additional volumes will follow "The Stormy Waves of Grief" and each will include another five weeks' worth of prayers and reflections. Together, the three volumes will allow you to pray through my entire litany.

INTRODUCTION

Praying the Litany

You can pray through the devotional however you wish, beginning on the first day or in the middle of any given month, or on the first day of your cycle.

I wrote the litany for both individual and small group use. If you know of others experiencing the pain of infertility, consider praying about inviting them to pray through the devotional with you. I've personally found hearing about the journeys of others to be helpful, and have learned from their wisdom and experience. You also never know what encouragement and support you might offer someone else through praying together and sharing your own story.

Have your Bible handy. There are several references to Scripture in the reflections. You'll also want to have paper or a journal and something to write down your answers to reflection questions as well as to put into words newly discovered feelings or questions, which you can bring to confession or discuss with a spiritual director.

This leads to my next point: I've written this devotional from my personal experience and background. I'm a Catholic Christian, so my experience comes from living the traditions and teachings of the Catholic Church. You don't need to be Catholic to pray through this devotional, but I want you to be aware that I reference teachings specific to the Catholic Church, like the Sacrament of Reconciliation or going to confession. If you have questions, I encourage you to learn more about what the Catholic Church teaches and why. You can start at the website for the U.S. Conference of Catholic Bishops[2], at *usccb.org*. If you're not interested in the details of the Catholic faith, that's fine, too. Christians of all backgrounds share many of the same basic beliefs, so you'll be able to easily identify with most, if not all, of the included prayers in this litany.

Please know that sharing this litany with you is very personal to me. It makes me vulnerable to the opinions and even criticisms

---

2 *www.usccb.org/beliefs-and-teachings/what-we-believe/*

of those who will learn the struggles and temptations to sin that I've been living through for so long. But even with this fear of opening up myself for others to judge, I know God is calling me to share my litany, and my journey, with others who are suffering similar experiences.

Infertility can cause great loneliness and a feeling of separation from loved ones, especially when no one seems to understand. Many people aren't able to verbalize their feelings, so I hope this prayer helps you recognize your own struggles and begin the process of healing. Don't beat yourself up too much if you see yourself struggling with many of these same issues—they all came to my own mind when I was writing this litany. Give yourself some grace, and have increased hope and faith in God's desire to heal you, if not physically, definitely spiritually, emotionally and mentally.

I also invite you to join the Facebook community for Sarah's Hope & Abraham's Promise, at *facebook.com/shapministry*, and connect online with other women and men who have struggled with infertility. You may also visit our website, at *hopeforinfertility.com*, to learn more about this ministry I helped start to serve couples struggling with infertility and pregnancy loss, as well as those touched by adoption. You'll find resources to help you on your own fertility journey and stories of other couples to inspire you. I'd also love to hear from you.

May the love of the Father, fellowship of the Son and wisdom of the Holy Spirit be with you as you pray through this litany. Be honest with yourself and have courage! God will give you the strength you need to follow His will.

JENNIFER CROWLEY

A LITANY FOR WOMEN STRUGGLING WITH INFERTILITY

Lord, have mercy. R. Lord, have mercy.
Christ, have mercy. R. Christ, have mercy.
Lord, have mercy. R. Lord, have mercy.

From the spirit of despair, **Deliver me, Lord.**
From the sin of despairing against hope,
From the temptation to give into weariness,
From the temptation to believe this cross is more than I can bear,
From the temptation to believe I somehow deserve this cross,
From the inability to see beauty in my life,
From the temptation to doubt I will ever feel joy,
From the spirit of selfishness,
From the temptation to grasp, control and demand,
From the temptation to feel hurt when my loved ones fail to ask about my infertility struggle,
From the temptation to feel excluded when I'm not invited to child-centered events,
From the temptation to make others' pregnancies about my not being pregnant,
From the temptation to display poor body language around others who have been blessed with children,
From the temptation to dismiss others' struggles as trivial compared to my own,
From the spirit of envy,
From the resentment I feel toward others who do not struggle with infertility,
From the temptation to silently scoff at those who speak of timing their pregnancies at their convenience,

From the temptation to discourage those who speak of their ideal plan to grow their family,

From the temptation to react poorly when someone announces a pregnancy,

From the temptation to get frustrated when women who have been blessed with children dwell on their pregnancies or on stories about their children,

From the temptation to flaunt the freedom my child-free life offers while in the presence of others with children,

From the spirit of anger,

From the temptation to obsess over my struggles with infertility,

From the temptation to complain,

From impatience,

From the temptation to be quick to take offense,

From the temptation to pursue every solution to infertility the world presents without pause to consider the consequences,

From being quick to judge the decisions of others about the way they pursue, or choose not to pursue, building their family,

From the spirit of faithlessness,

From the sin of self-pity when I ask, "Why me?"

From the temptation to believe I am not woman enough because I'm unable to conceive,

From the sin of blasphemy,

From the sin of ingratitude,

From the paralysis generated by stunted dreams and hopes too small,

From the lack of trust that You love me and that I'm worthy,

For the grace of temperance, **Please grant it, Lord.**
For the grace to offer up all sorrows,
For an increase in hope, especially on Cycle Day 1,
For an increase in the fruit of the spirit that is peace, especially at the beginning of a new cycle,
For an increase in the fruit of the spirit that is joy, especially at the beginning of a new cycle,
For the grace to be positive and committed,
For the grace to be patient and persevering,
For the healing of my body, the fertility diseases that plague it, and the restoration of full health to my reproductive system,
For the grace to be free from chronic stress,
For the gift of children,
For the gift of conception,
For the gift of bearing healthy children,
For the grace to dream and hope big,
For the gift of supportive loved ones,
For the spirit of discernment to seek God's will with every treatment option and family building decision,
For the grace to cherish and celebrate both the unitive and procreative meanings of the marriage act,
For an increase in trust and casting out of all fear,
For an increase in respect for the sanctity of life,
For an increase in the use of Natural Family Planning around the world,
For the desire to draw closer to You in prayer,
For the grace to be open to Your will for this cycle and be set free from my expectations,
For an increase in trust to replace all feelings of chaos and confusion when infertility treatments don't result in conception,
For my feelings of blame and criticism to be replaced with acceptance and hope,

For an increase in humility and casting out of all shame,
For an increase in the fruits of the Holy Spirit that are love, joy, peace, generosity, faithfulness, gentleness and self-control when someone announces a pregnancy,
For the grace to forgive those who have wounded me through this infertility struggle, whether the wounds were intentional or unintentional,
For the grace to be compassionate, loving and kind,
For the grace to put myself in others' shoes,
For the grace to praise You for the gift of life You've granted to our loved ones,
For the grace to increase in holiness,
For this cross of infertility to strengthen my marriage and draw me and my spouse closer to You and one another,
For the grace to embrace Your gift of the cross of infertility,
For the grace to recognize and embrace all areas of my life that need my time and attention,
For the grace to be merciful to myself,
For the grace to increase in holy indifference,
For acceptance of where I am on my infertility journey,
For the gift of faith in knowing that You can turn all things, even my infertility, into good,
For the grace to forgive any resentments I have toward my spouse for our infertility,
For the grace to forgive myself for my infertility,
For the grace to forgive You for my infertility,
For the courage to address and work through the grief from my infertility so that I may find healing,
For this cross of infertility to sanctify me, and thereby help me to become the saint You've called me to become,
For the spirit of discernment to know when to take breaks in actively trying to conceive,
For the spirit of discernment to know if the time should come for us to end all active treatments in trying to conceive,

For the spirit of discernment in seeking Your will for the future of our family,
For the gift of both a support community as well as trusted and faithful loved ones through whom You would use to speak to me about Your will for me,
For the openness to explore our call to using the path of adoption to build our family,
For the grace to die to myself and that You would open my heart to Your will for our family,
For the gift of open communication with my spouse and that we be in agreement about our family building journey,
For the desire to actively seek and recognize the work of the Holy Spirit in my life,
For the grace to witness to You by word and example,
For the grace to use Your gift of the cross of infertility to build Your Kingdom,
For the grace to embrace my call to spiritual motherhood,
For the grace to recognize opportunities to love and serve others,
For the openness to allowing Your grace to bear fruit in my life through my infertility,
For the desire to contribute my time, talent and treasure to building Your Kingdom,
For all of those who struggle with infertility,
hear their prayers, Lord.
For those whose children You have called home,
please comfort them, Lord.
For those who remain childless,
grant them fruitfulness and peace in their vocation, Lord.
For those with unsupportive spouses or loved ones,
bring to them a community of support, Lord.
For increased awareness of the cross of infertility throughout the Church and world, please grant it, Lord.

For those who promote a culture of life, please bless them, Lord.

For those who minister to couples suffering from infertility, bless them and bring them couples who most need to receive Your love and hear the beauty of Your truth, Lord.

In thanksgiving for being called to the vocation of marriage, **Praise God!**

In thanksgiving for my parents saying "yes" to the gift of children,

In thanksgiving for the gift of children granted to our loved ones,

In thanksgiving for all of the miraculous ways my body lives, moves and breathes,

In thanksgiving for those who minister to me,

In thanksgiving for the gift of faith,

In thanksgiving for Your love, constant presence, mercy and strength,

(*Your patron saint's name*), **Pray for us.**

(*Your spouse's patron saint's name*),

St. Gerard Majella, patron saint of women who hope to conceive,

Sts. Anne and Joachim, patron saints for couples struggling with infertility,

St. Rita, patroness of impossible causes and hopeless circumstances,

St. Jude, patron saint of desperate cases and lost causes,

All you holy men and women,

All you angels and saints,

St. Michael the Archangel, protect us…

Amen.

OH YOU OF LITTLE FAITH,
why did you doubt?

WEEK 1

Prayers Seeking Freedom from Waves of Hopelessness

From Despair to Hope

Reaching another Cycle Day 1 is heartbreaking when you're trying to conceive. I've often avoided trips to the bathroom when my menstrual cycle is supposed to start, not wanting to shatter my hopes of conceiving. Wanting instead to believe my husband and I were pregnant—not face any signs of the alternative.

When I'd find out that God had not willed a pregnancy for us that month, all I could do was reel in my sadness and criticize the world and God for being unfair. The despair I felt, and can still feel, seemed unbearable.

This first week of the devotional allows us to grieve while relying on God, even attempting to unite our suffering with the Passion of Christ.

Come back to this first week whenever you reach a Cycle Day 1 to give yourself space to mourn. Be gentle with yourself. Experience the emotions that arise, but try to release them to God so they don't begin to control your life and your ability to be fruitful. As often as it takes, whether it's every hour or 10 minutes, surrender your despair and ask God to shower you with hope instead. My prayers are with you.

> *This first week of the devotional allows us to grieve while relying on God...*

Week 1: Prayers Seeking Freedom from Waves of Hopelessness

DAY 1

From the spirit of despair, deliver me, Lord...

Cycle Day 1 is always the most difficult day. It marks the passing of another month of trying to achieve pregnancy on days you thought you might be fertile then waiting for a few weeks after ovulation to see what your efforts might bring. You allowed yourself, sometimes unconsciously, to get your hopes up, maybe seeing physical symptoms, like fatigue, nausea or headaches as an early sign of pregnancy. You may have had an unusually long cycle and courageously bought an over-the-counter pregnancy test. But now, it's Cycle Day 1—another sorrowful reminder of what is not yet in God's plans for this chapter of your life.

Many times, I've succumbed to the hope that I might be pregnant, only to meet despair a few days later. I once had a positive over-the-counter pregnancy test, only to have a negative blood test the next day. During those 24 hours, my husband and I allowed ourselves to get caught up in the emotions we had longed to experience for years. The reality of realizing that it had been yet another unsuccessful cycle was heartbreaking.

The ease with which the spirit of despair can overtake someone with infertility on Cycle Day 1 is always immense and difficult to escape. For most of us, the pain of infertility will be the most significant we've had to experience. It's a death of our dreams or a "no" or "not yet" to our prayers—and it's on repeat every 30 days or so for an unknown period of time. Six months? A year? Several years? Decades? Forever? The many unknowns of infertility allow for little closure. We stumble between finding a glimmer of hope for the next cycle and accepting that we may never get pregnant, an occurrence that ends with our cycles when we reach menopause.

This despair affects us, body, mind and spirit. Along with painful periods, uncomfortable bloating, intense cramping and headaches that force us to shut out the world, we also grieve the passing of time, another month when we've not yet been able to conceive the children for whom we long.

During these times, we must pray for deliverance from the spirit of despair and ask for God's grace to continue having hope in and acceptance of His plan.

So, especially on Cycle Day 1, those of us facing this cross must be kind to ourselves. I found the best way to avoid the full onslaught of despair was to plan a healthy "reward." For every Cycle Day 1, I arranged something that I could look forward to—a kind of silver lining to having not yet conceived. A couple's massage, a special dinner, a gathering of trusted friends, an adventurous activity, permission to binge watch my favorite TV show for an evening. Allowing ourselves the space to grieve is important, but so is filling our lives with the many things that bring us joy.

Reflections

1. At this point in your family building journey, what emotion consumes you the most on Cycle Day 1?

2. What activity or experience might you (and your spouse) enjoy at the start of a new cycle to help ease the disappointment?

3. Reflect on Psalm 30:6b, which refers to the ending of one thing, one chapter, and the beginning of another. How might this verse help you with the disappointment that comes with the ending of another cycle?

Week 1: Prayers Seeking Freedom from Waves of Hopelessness

DAY 2

From the sin of despairing against hope, deliver me, Lord...

When I hear the term "despair," I'm oftentimes reminded of a scene in the 1985 TV film adaptation of "Anne of Green Gables," which I watched over and over again as a child. Anne's rebuked for saying she's in the "depths of despair" because, according to Marilla, the woman who had taken Anne in, that means you've turned your back on God.

That seemingly random reference helps me remember the seriousness of what being truly hopeless means. To despair against hope means we no longer believe God has our best interests in mind, and we doubt that He has the power to turn this heartache into something good (Rom 8:28). To despair against hope is tragic indeed.

According to the Catholic Encyclopedia at *newadvent.org*, "… [despair against hope] contravenes with a special directness certain attributes of Almighty God, such as His goodness, mercy, and faith-keeping…its power for working harm in the human soul is fundamentally far greater than other sins inasmuch as it cuts off the way of escape and those who fall under its spell are frequently, as a matter of fact, found to surrender themselves unreservedly to all sorts of sinful indulgence."

In other words, despairing against hope is a gateway to a playground of sin that has a domino effect. To sin means to "miss the mark," with the mark being God's love. When we begin to despair, we invite in emotions or build bigger walls that prevent us from feeling God's love. We soon dig a hole with little escape in sight. The times I doubted God was my refuge and strength, and further doubted He could bring me to a greater place in time, I also found resisting the near occasion of other sin almost impossible— deepening my hole of despair.

Discerning which way to focus our hope is difficult. But whatever the focus, we can't allow ourselves to lose that hope, despair or turn our backs on God. He is greater than we often believe Him to be, and He isn't ignorant of our heart's deepest desires. Anything is possible! As my husband says, "Don't put God in a box!"

Hold fast to hope, for it anchors us and holds us steady in any storm. We don't know where our infertility will lead. But focusing on Him, regardless of the outcome, will carry us to the other side, where we'll find peace, joy and comfort in the surrender to His great and beautiful plan for us. He longs to bless us with this plan, which will bring us to the fullness of our salvation—and allow us to rest in Him.

Reflections

1. When have you felt most hopeless during this struggle, and what were the circumstances?

2. It's difficult to maintain hope when our focus of hope is on a specific, unknown outcome. Instead, our focus of hope must be on God. Remembering a time when you felt most hopeless, imagine yourself focusing on God, on feeling His love and comfort. Does this lift some of your despair?

3. Reflect on 2 Corinthians 4:7-18, and imagine St. Paul's encouragement to the people of Corinth is addressed to you, about your struggle with infertility. How do his words make you feel?

Week 1: Prayers Seeking Freedom from Waves of Hopelessness

DAY 3

From the temptation to give into weariness, deliver me, Lord...

Does this sound familiar? Your period has started and you're feeling a flood of emotions—disappointment, anger, sadness, frustration and confusion. You allow yourself to experience this cluster of feelings, bouncing from one emotion to the next. You go from wanting to cry to wanting to pick a fight with whomever crosses your path—anything to release these feelings.

You have to immediately let your doctor know that you didn't conceive so you can discuss the plan for the new cycle. Oftentimes, medication has to be taken within the first three to five days, leaving little time to mourn the "death" of this past cycle. Before you know it, you've geared up for trying to conceive this cycle. You and your spouse attempt to push down all of those resurfaced negative feelings so you can find hope and positivity in praying that this cycle will be the one where you conceive the miracle baby you've been praying for.

You track every day of your cycle, taking medications as scheduled and noting your body's signs of fertility. Maybe you have bloodwork drawn on particular days or a series of pelvic ultrasounds to follow how your body is responding as the cycle progresses. When it looks to be about the time of ovulation, you and your husband make sure to "use" those days to try to conceive. It's no longer the stuff of romance novels. Spontaneity and fun have been replaced with pressure and expectations. Not exactly the atmosphere married couples deserve and are privileged to enjoy.

Then, as your cycle progresses and different medications are required, you continue to do your part to stick to this cycle's plan of trying to conceive. It's during these times that you're filled with anticipation and hope as you wait to see if conception has occurred.

You do your best to not make assumptions about every little thing your body does, thinking it may be an early sign of pregnancy, but then you can't help yourself from searching the internet for proof. If the internet says so, then it must be true.

Then, it happens—you start to spot. Panic sets in, but still, you wonder if it could be implantation bleeding and not your actual period looming around the corner. This may go on for a day or two or three, until it's clear that your period has begun, and you're back to Cycle Day 1. Or maybe you have no spotting and are feeling super positive and excited until a visit to the bathroom drags you to your knees. You discover Mother Nature didn't play nice and trying to conceive has failed. Again. That flood of emotions returns, and you pick up the phone to call your doctor to report the news. Again. Repeat the entire cycle. Again. And again. And again.

This is exhausting. Just writing about it has exhausted me, and I'm quite confident that no one struggling with infertility would disagree. There's no fun in the sheer number of doctor's appointments, in the different medications and their side effects of weight gain, insomnia and emotional instability that leads to regular bouts of crying, irritability and mood swings. The anxiety that all of these efforts may never result in a pregnancy builds up and further exhausts you.

In a different situation, this degree of fatigue would bring me to my spouse and I would depend on him to lift me up. Alas, marriages going through infertility are further complicated by the fact that spouses often have their own varying depths of sadness mixed with the occasional sliver of hope. Neither spouse can rely on the other to pull them out of the pit, for they are right there themselves.

With each cycle, I try to manage my extreme emotions while simultaneously being attentive to my marriage and my relationship with my husband—outside of trying to conceive. Building a healthy marriage takes effort when no hardships are present, but when both spouses feel deadened and overwhelmed by infertility, maintaining a healthy marital relationship can seem draining.

Unfortunately, I've witnessed infertility break marriages apart. It's tragic.

The temptation to give in to all-out weariness is very real. My weariness is always present, lingering just under the surface of my "I'm fine" smile. It's been so easy to look at my situation and its exasperatingly never-ending cycle, and want to give up or give in. I often cry out to God and scream that I don't have it in me to continue. But then there is the stillness—the stillness I hear in His reply that tells me, "I have the strength for everything through Him who empowers me" (Phil 4:13). Or I am reminded of Jacob's well: "Jacob's well was there, and so Jesus, wearied as He was with His journey, sat down beside the well. It was about the sixth hour. There came a woman of Samaria to draw water. Jesus said to her, 'Give me a drink'" (Jn 4:6-7). In one of Pope Francis' homilies during World Youth Day 2019, our Holy Father talked specifically of this Scripture passage: "The Gospel we have heard does not shrink from showing us Jesus, wearied from His journey. At midday, when the sun makes all its strength and power felt, we encounter Him beside the well. He needed to relieve and quench His thirst, to refresh His steps, to recover His strength in order to continue His mission…The Lord knew what it was to be tired, and in His weariness so many struggles of our nations and peoples, our communities and all who are weary and heavily burdened can find a place."

> *"The Gospel we have heard does not shrink from showing us Jesus, wearied from His journey."*

I, too, "thirst." My weariness has left me dry and parched. However, I consider Christ's thirst in this Scripture passage and imagine His weariness, not just at the well but through a life of ministry that would ultimately lead to His Passion on the cross. I remember the many times He would retreat alone to pray, to regain strength for His calling, to find rest and rejuvenation. He has felt my weariness; He feels it now and is calling me into deeper prayer with Him to regain that strength needed for my own journey.

"Come to me, all you who labor and are burdened, and I will give you rest. Take my yoke upon you and learn from me, for I am meek and humble of heart; and you will find rest for yourselves. For my yoke is easy, and my burden light" (Mt 11:28-30).

Reflections

1. Trying to conceive, whether it be for a few months or for more than 10 years, can feel as though we've been laboring and are burdened. Some rest would be nice. What does that rest look like to you? In what ways can you imagine finding rest even during this trial of trying to conceive?

2. What specifically makes you feel weary on your infertility journey? Can you think of ways that might relieve some of it? Have you discussed these feelings of weariness with your spouse, a trusted loved one or a counselor? See if naming aloud those particular aspects of your journey might spark some ideas about how to overcome the temptation to grow weary.

3. Discernment is also an important part of the infertility journey. For many, there's a point when a couple decides to discontinue (or take a break from) fertility treatments and attempt to find peace with God's plan, whatever it may look like. Their decision to lay down this cross may come after experiencing negative physical, emotional, psychological and spiritual effects. Have you and your spouse discussed a timeline for how long you both feel willing to continue the journey of actively trying to conceive? What might lead you to feel it's time to surrender this struggle?

Week 1: Prayers Seeking Freedom from Waves of Hopelessness

DAY 4

From the temptation to believe this cross is more than I can bear, deliver me, Lord …

"God will never give you more than you can handle!"

I've heard this too many times to count throughout my struggles with infertility. This common phrase of encouragement, one I often use myself, is supposed to offer hope and support to loved ones going through difficult circumstances.

Not to contradict pop-culture proverbs, but I've felt many times that my infertility journey is more than I can handle. I've also felt completely consumed by the entire struggle and all that comes along with it.

While I watched everyone around me become pregnant—multiple times—over the past 10-plus years, I've often felt like I was barely holding on, treading water as I try to keep my head above the surface, as the world of happy families swims along in the direction I deeply long to go.

It's interesting that I imagine myself like this, almost drowning, when I am so drawn to "The Walking on the Water" Scripture passage in the Gospel of Matthew. (You may want to reread the full passage, Matthew 14:22-33, in your Bible or the Author's Note.) Peter is confident at first, trusting Jesus as he gets out of the boat to walk to Him. But then Peter, distracted, takes his eyes off the Lord and loses sight of what he's doing. He notices the tumultuousness around him, the busyness, the fear. He starts to sink.

Those of us struggling with infertility often experience panic, overwhelming anxiety, restlessness, fear of the future and helplessness. The suffering—the cross of infertility—feels like too much to bear. We sink into that mindset and cry out, "Lord, save me!"

As He raises us to comfort us, He asks, "O you of little faith, why did you doubt?"

He has been with us the whole time. Only with Him can we get through this. Even though it may not always feel like it, St. Paul was correct in his First Epistle to the Corinthians. God will not let you be tried beyond your strength, and He will provide "a way out" so that we can bear the sufferings that come our way (1 Cor 10:13). However, we have to be willing to see His way by keeping our eyes on Him.

So, instead of focusing on the cold, sterile stirrups of the doctor's office, another prick of the needle drawing blood or a friend's upcoming pregnancy announcement, I try to keep my eyes on Jesus and have confidence in His presence.

I may not know now how my infertility journey will ultimately end, or how this journey may change me, but if I remember that God has not forsaken me, that He won't let me be tried beyond my strength, I'll be able to go, with hope, where He's leading me. He'll provide a way for me to bear the suffering and do what seems impossible. Maybe even "walk on water."

Reflections

1. What triggers you into feeling like the cross of infertility has become too much to bear? Can you recall a time when you truly felt like you were sinking and might not recover from the whole infertility experience?

2. What "ways out" has God given you to help you bear the cross of infertility?

3. A quick prayer to offer up in those moments when we feel overwhelmed and slipping more deeply into our grief is to simply say, "Lord, save me!" as St. Peter did. You might find it soothing to repeat it over and over, like in Taizé prayer[3] or as a meditative mantra. Consider praying "Lord, save me!" in this way the next time you feel fear creeping in, and everything begins to feel too heavy to bear.

---

[3] The contemplative prayer form that has become known as "Taizé Prayer" takes its name from the Taizé Community of France, an ecumenical religious community that uses singing or chanting of simple musical phrases. The chants are repeated over and over, similar to a mantra or praying the Rosary, with the purpose of quieting the mind and heart in order that the song may become prayer. *www.taize.fr/en*

Week 1: Prayers Seeking Freedom from Waves of Hopelessness

DAY 5

From the temptation to believe I somehow deserve this cross, deliver me, Lord...

I deserve this. I've made so many mistakes. I've given in to temptation more than I care to admit.

These have often been my thoughts. So many of us who struggle with infertility believe we somehow deserve this cross, that we're being punished for past sins or poor decisions we made as a young adult. We reexamine every small stain on our past behaviors. We wonder if we are "good enough" to be a parent, and we doubt if we are "worthy enough" of God's blessings.

This self-evaluation may lead us to believe that we haven't done enough for God. How often have I skipped Mass, failed to dive deeper into my faith or turned my eyes away from injustices in need of my voice? We may also think back on all the times we engaged in sex hoping to not get pregnant, or for some among us, on a past elective abortion, when we actively chose to not parent when given the opportunity.

Placing blame on something or someone, including ourselves, isn't uncommon in the stages of grieving our infertility. But nothing could be further from the truth. Even couples with explainable causes for their infertility that can be attributed to a past behavior don't deserve this. None of us do.

However, in our minds, the sins we've stacked on one side of a scale have grown so heavy that we can't imagine being granted any kind of blessing—and it's all our own doing. We believe we have the control, the ability to create the gift of new life. But this control doesn't exist. Just as many women with our same "sins," "diseases" or "consequences" have conceived, others without poor decisions in their past remain unable to conceive. Again, I have to reiterate, we don't deserve this! We're not being punished.

Infertility just happens. It's what God has allowed us to experience for reasons we may never know.

In the Gospel of John, Jesus challenges this view of "karma." "As [Jesus] passed by he saw a man blind from birth. His disciples asked him, 'Rabbi, who sinned, this man or his parents, that he was born blind?' Jesus answered, 'Neither he nor his parents sinned; it is so that the works of God might be made visible through him'" (Jn 9:1-3).

Jesus explains that God allowed the man to suffer blindness, not because he "deserved" the impairment for past sins, but because it could give glory to God in some way. Similarly, our infertility hasn't been handed to us because of any sins of ours, our husband's or our parents'. Again, it's not something we "deserve" or have done to ourselves.

Everyone experiences suffering—it's an inescapable part of living in an imperfect world. We don't get to choose our crosses. True, infertility is a large, heavy and tremendous cross. But it's also true that "the works of God may be made visible through [us]."

God is merciful, not vengeful, and He seeks opportunities to bless us, even in our suffering. We have to put aside the lie that we deserve this cross and instead believe in His greatest truth: We are loved just as we are, with all of our current and past sins. We are His precious, beloved daughters, and He wants goodness for us.

> *We have to put aside the lie that we deserve this cross and instead believe in His greatest truth: We are loved just as we are, with all of our current and past sins.*

Reflections

1. Have you ever felt as though you didn't deserve to conceive and bear a child? Or do you ever feel as though you don't deserve to be a mother at all, to any children you might be blessed with, whether through conception or adoption? Where does this belief come from?

2. Have you caught yourself finding reasons to blame yourself or your husband for your infertility? Did that bring you or your marriage peace? Why have you tried to place blame for your suffering?

3. Reflect on 2 Corinthians 12:7-9a. See how the Lord responds to St. Paul's plea for an end to his suffering for a "thorn in the flesh," which some theologians say is a sickness or physical disability. Place yourself in this scene, pouring your heart out to God, expressing your despair and incredible grief from the suffering of infertility. Imagine begging Him to lift this heavy cross of infertility from you. How does He respond? What if His response to you is the same as to St. Paul? How do you answer?

Week 1: Prayers Seeking Freedom from Waves of Hopelessness

DAY 6

From the inability to see beauty in my life, deliver me, Lord...

Everything seems cloaked in darkness when you're treading the waves of infertility. Tears from pain and mourning cloud your vision, often convincing you that God has forgotten you. Your gaze, so fixed on conceiving, blurs the goodness and blessings in your life—the beauty all around you in the present.

For me, this darkness was all-consuming. Ignoring the gifts in my life only plunged me further into the abyss of sadness from this heavy cross of infertility. I discovered that the only way to get through this journey with a hopeful heart was to open my eyes and see the beauty in the present moment. Once I was able to realize the little gifts in the everyday, my heart found it easier to also recognize hope and to regain the trust in God that He has, in fact, not forgotten about me.

I believe He tries to remind us of His presence in our lives by gifting us little signs of beauty and precious experiences all of the time. I jot down these "God moments" in a journal to return to when I feel the darkness creeping back in.

Recognizing my marriage and my family as blessings was far easier than actually feeling those blessings. So, I focused on being mindful of the little things happening in the present moment. For example, I love wind chimes. I love hearing the unique melody created when the metal rods clink against one another in the breeze. When I come across chimes, I close my eyes and feel the beauty in that moment. Allowing the chimes to capture my mind takes away thoughts of infertility, at least temporarily.

Once I recognized this power, I began intentionally bringing beauty into the mundane moments of my life. I have a big window in my home office where I love to gaze and appreciate God's creation—beauty He has placed even outside the walls of my own home. This became, and remains, where I purposefully go to address my daily to-do list, making even the mundane task enchanting and mesmerizing.

This is similar to the practice of mindfulness, of finding beauty in the small things. When I take a walk, instead of fretting about all of the things I have to do to address infertility or throwing angry thoughts around in my mind, I actually look at the bark of the trees, the shape and color of the clouds in the sky, the individual blades of grass. I intentionally listen to the sounds of the squirrels scurrying along the tree branches or hear the birds chirping. Focusing deeply on something besides infertility lightens my mind and heart, even if only for a minute. And every minute is significant, with each second of peace adding to the positive effect on my overall health and well-being.

When life feels especially dreary and the weight of the infertility journey robs me of awe or wonder, I close my eyes, breathe deeply, then reopen them with the anticipation that I can find beauty once again.

If I look for it, I'll find awe. I'll find wonder. I'll find beauty in the world around me—in nature, absolutely, but also in the people God has placed in my life, our interactions and their support of my family building journey. I look for beauty especially in my spouse, and I ask God to help me recognize His beauty in my life.

And when I find beauty, I try to hold on to it for as long as possible. The little things truly are awe-inspiring and full of wonder. But the true miracle is peace of mind.

Reflections

1. Do you struggle with being able to see beauty in your life?

2. When the burdensome weight of deep sadness from longing to conceive drags you down, pulls you underwater, do you find yourself wanting to give in? Give up? How might recognizing the beauty in your life, the gifts and experiences granted to you, help pull you out of this sinking feeling and have hope in God's plan for your family?

3. Reflect on Luke 12:27. Jesus references the beauty of nature in something as small as a single flower. Make a list of how you see and feel beauty in your life, and keep it accessible, such as on a smartphone, for easy reference on the go and during the first week of each cycle.

Week 1: Prayers Seeking Freedom from Waves of Hopelessness

DAY 7

From the temptation to doubt I will ever feel joy, deliver me, Lord...

Infertility not only dims the light at the end of the proverbial tunnel, but it also barricades us in. The idea of truly feeling joy, especially if you've struggled with infertility for many years, can almost seem foreign.

In the beginning of our infertility journey, when my husband and I were most actively trying to conceive, I remember being almost hyperalert. I tried to never to miss a beat in our plan to conceive—from medications to doctor's appointments—because timing is everything when you're trying to get pregnant. But this heightened state of awareness didn't leave much room for joy in my life.

Many of us lack hope of ever feeling the joy we are so desperately trying to find. Burdened by the weight of our pain that seems to suffocate us with every passing cycle, we give in to cynicism and allow the possibility of joy to be a distant memory.

In Proverbs, we learn, "A joyful heart is the health of the body, but a depressed spirit dries up the bones" (Prv 17:22). Well, obviously! I know what it's like to have dry bones—I'm often referred to as "barren." But how can I find joy with those big "what ifs?" What if I never conceive a child? What if I'm never able to experience the miracle of pregnancy? Or what if I never become a parent, either through conception or adoption? Is a joyful heart ever possible?

> "A joyful heart is the health of the body, but a depressed spirit dries up the bones" (Prv 17:22).

No one knows what the future holds. I pray for all of us that it brings a healthy pregnancy, maybe multiple pregnancies, and an abundance of precious children to raise to love the Lord! But the truth is, some of us will never experience pregnancy, which is probably difficult to read right now.

At the time this book is published, I'll be more than 10 years into my infertility journey. Although many of the reflections were written early in my journey, this particular reflection was written more recently, after I was diagnosed with premature menopause at the "ripe old age" of 37. This diagnosis feels like someone has robbed me of my chance of ever conceiving. EVER. While my husband and I had hoped for about seven more years of trying to conceive, my reproductive organs gave up on me with no warning. Our hopes were quickly taken away.

What I want to share about my premature menopause diagnosis is the joy I've experienced, even when the reality of never conceiving became apparent. The joy wasn't visible at first. I had to hope for it and be confident in its possibility, despite this enormous hole inside my chest. But joy gradually found its way to my heart as that hole was filled—not with the experience but rather with my purpose.

Every life has a purpose. We each have a specific set of skills or experiences that allow us to affect the world. For those of us who listen and try to hear the purpose God is calling us to, I believe we will find abundant joy upon taking His chosen path.

My joy is in serving others who also find themselves in this great struggle. This book is part of my healing and also part of my joy. The founding of Sarah's Hope & Abraham's Promise, an infertility support ministry, has been my joy. I may have never been pregnant, but I've been fruitful. And to bear fruit, in whichever way God is calling, not only fills our lives with sweetness but also enlightens the lives of those around us. Our fruit becomes sustenance for many: "Its leaves were beautiful, its fruit abundant, providing food for all. Under it the wild beasts found shade, in its branches the birds of the air nested; all flesh ate of it" (Dn 4:9).

Reflections

1. Have you doubted that you will ever feel joy after this difficult time of your life? Do you despair? Do any particular situations trigger these feelings?

2. Is pregnancy the only means by which you feel you can find joy?

3. Reflect on John 15:1-11, paying special attention to the final verse, when Jesus says, "I have told you this so that my joy may be in you and your joy may be complete." Can you hear Jesus telling you this? He wants us to be close to Him, to unite our will with His so, through Him, we're able to bear fruit. He wants our joy to be complete. Can you believe this?

4. Do you place conditions on Jesus, that you will only feel joy if a specific thing happens? What will it take for you to trust Jesus and His promise of complete joy, regardless of your fertility outcome?

5. *(Trigger warning: If you're not yet ready to imagine what your life might look like without conceiving, return to this reflection on another day, if you feel called.)* Can you imagine your future without ever being able to conceive? What does it look like to you? Are you open to other ways of answering your call to the vocation of motherhood, such as adoption or spiritual motherhood? How might this scenario bring you joy? To open your eyes to the possibility of finding joy without a pregnancy, consider talking to other women who intentionally practice spiritual motherhood or who chose to adopt. Learn how they recognize and embrace joy from those callings.

Closing Week 1 with Hope

Lord, this is the most difficult week for me. Month after month, I find myself right back here and feel as if I can't recover or move on. Help me move forward. Help me surrender this despair.

Deliver me.

Wherever I was marked by despair, fill me instead with Your hope. Cast my gaze toward You rather than on a specific outcome. Help me to keep You as my focus so that I may realize the extent of my strength and power to endure. Give me the confidence to know that I will not grow weary, that when I'm falling, I'll feel Your arms carrying me. Allow me to fully feel Your presence so guilt will not weigh me down and I'll once again realize all of the beauty in my life. Envelop me with confidence in the promise of joy.

Lord, I'm letting go. The despair is falling and my hope in You is rising. Be near me and bless me.

Amen.

WEEK 2

Prayers Seeking Freedom from Waves of Egotism

From Selfishness to Graciousness

Pope Francis has warned us to beware of our own egos. In a June 2018 address to the Pontifical Academy for Life General Assembly, our Holy Father emphasized, "Behind the indifference toward human life lies a contagious illness that blinds people to the challenges and struggles of others…Like the mythical figure Narcissus, people risk becoming infected by a 'contagious spiritual virus' that turns them into 'mirrored men and women who only see themselves and nothing else.'"[4]

In other words, inflated egos leave us at risk of becoming so solely focused on ourselves and our own well-being that we're blinded to the challenges and struggles of others. I dare say, not taking notice of the state of those around us is a serious attack on the very mission of Christianity itself.

St. Paul, in his Letter to the Philippians, implores us to "…humbly regard others as more important than yourselves, each looking out not for his own interests, but [also] everyone for those of others" (Phil 2:3b-4). St. Paul encourages us to model Christ, who showed us how to live for others and demonstrated humility and love throughout His life here on earth.

Week 2's daily prayers focus on the deliverance from our own egos. Given how all-consuming infertility is, it's understandable that big emotions overwhelm us, turning our focus inward toward our own pain, while simultaneously being oblivious to the pain of

---

4 Junno Arocho Esteves. "Narcissism is a spiritual virus, says Pope Francis." Catholic Herald, June 26, 2018, *catholicherald.co.uk/news/2018/06/26/narcissism-is-a-spiritual-virus-says-pope-francis.*

others. This self-focus hurt loved ones in my life and left me more isolated on my infertility journey. We all long to feel connected and cared for on our journeys. Ironically, by turning my gaze outward toward others, I lifted myself up.

With these prayers, I ask for graciousness to enter your heart. In the secular world, being gracious means to be kind, thoughtful and aware of others. But in the divine world, to be gracious is to be merciful, forgiving and compassionate. Graciousness provides the intimacy those struggling with infertility need. Come back to these reflections every time you feel alone or lonely. Allow Jesus to grant you the peace that comes from being freed from the focus on self so you may, once again, connect with others.

> ...in the divine world, to be gracious is to be merciful, forgiving and compassionate.

Week 2: Prayers Seeking Freedom from Waves of Egotism

DAY 8

From the spirit of selfishness, deliver me, Lord...

Why do we long to become mothers? I know this seems like a silly question, but, really, why does anyone want to have children? Is it just a natural progression for married couples? You get married, you spend time building a home together, you have children. You watch your children grow and then, hopefully, watch grandchildren grow as well.

As someone who has tried to conceive, unsuccessfully, for more than 10 years, I easily know my "why." I'd love to see my spouse's or my own physical features replicated in a child; to experience the joys—and even pains—of pregnancy and childbirth; to have the opportunity to help form a soul to love and serve God; to have a house filled with chaos, little feet and precious memories; to be able to relive the best moments of my own childhood through the eyes of a child; and, simply, to be so intimately connected to another human being.

Not only do those of us who long for children desire to see our families grow from the fruitfulness of the love we share in our marriage, children bring couples great joy in ways we also long to experience. These blessings from having children—and our desires—are all pure and good.

But after a long stretch of trying to conceive, darkness can enter one's soul. Honestly, during my own struggle, I've invited the darkness in at times. Infertility is painful, and I haven't always wanted, or been capable of, continually looking on the bright side. The repetitive cycle of hope followed with disappointment cracks open the door to thoughts that lead us away from God and the truths He has given us. Once on this path, being unable to conceive is suddenly more about why my needs and desires aren't being met rather than about missing out on the joy of becoming a mother.

At its essence, becoming a parent embodies selflessness. The act of creating a child begins with total self-giving to both God and your spouse. This self-giving is intended to be so complete that we focus on each other rather than what the end result may be—whether the fullness of love results in co-creating a child with our Lord. Yes, we acknowledge that any act might be creative as well as unitive, but, during the moment, selfless union with our spouse is the intent.

If the marital act brings a couple the gift of new life, that life began from total selflessness. It's our temptation toward selfishness that creeps into our minds when we begin to think we have a right to our own biological children. It's our temptation toward selfishness to use our children to affirm the self-worth we imagine comes from the gift of parenthood.

The pain of infertility is so great that it's easy, even understandable, for selfishness to creep in. It finds its way in when we're tempted to pursue unethical fertility treatments. It surfaces when we're resentful about hosting another baby shower for a friend. It's present when we think others should be more sensitive to our pain.

Selfishness was at my side the many times I became angry when loved ones talked about their growing families. I was selfish when I discounted my spouse's suffering. Because of my selfishness, I assumed his feelings were insignificant to my own.

Selfishness arises when we believe we are entitled to parenthood, and when we allow this suffering to consume our lives.

Infertility is so hard. Surviving this struggle without some selfishness would be nearly impossible. However, in my experience, the more I allow selfish thoughts to creep in or selfish actions to dictate my behavior, the more isolated, alone and angry

Every day, I ask for help in abandoning my selfishness so I can eventually find acceptance, connection and love.

I become. Every day, I ask for help in abandoning my selfishness so I can eventually find acceptance, connection and love.

Releasing our selfishness will ultimately make us the best parents and the most effective in our service to others.

Reflections

1. Do you see yourself being tempted toward selfishness? Is it in your own desire to have a child? In choosing fertility treatments? In relating—or not relating—to your spouse's suffering?

2. What are some ways you can break free of the self-focus that the struggle of infertility imparts?

3. Think of someone who lives a great example of being selfless in their struggles. What can you learn from them?

Week 2: Prayers Seeking Freedom from Waves of Egotism

DAY 9

From the temptation to grasp, control and demand, deliver me, Lord...

There's something incredibly beautiful about praying with hands outstretched toward God, ready to receive His will. As I've grown older, I've found myself needing to take this posture during my deepest moments of prayer. Throughout my infertility struggle, I've grasped and made demands of God, my spouse, friends and family, and even myself in an attempt to control the outcome of my journey. But praying in this posture allows me to undo the knots and tangles being controlling has created. I feel as if I'm letting go, surrendering and waiting to receive God's gift of joy and love.

Infertility leads many women to believe—to hope—that they have some degree of control over conceiving or carrying a baby to a healthy term. An inordinate amount of responsibility is laid on women who are trying to conceive, from adhering to medication regimens, recognizing and noting fertility signs and timing intercourse at the optimal time of their cycles, to maintaining prescribed diets and dealing with numerous medical appointments.

We fall into the trap of believing that if we just do everything we're supposed to do, we'll become pregnant. We exhaust ourselves, often at the expense of our health. Unfortunately, we can do everything right and still not conceive.

My life outside of infertility felt very put together. I've always been organized, with a plan for success for whatever I take on. Wanting so badly to conceive but being unable to make it happen, no matter what I tried, left me feeling like a failure—as though I'd somehow missed a step. Why else would this happen? Maybe if I just tried this method, ate that diet, did these exercises or saw that doctor, it would happen. I made demands of God. I tried reasoning with Him, blatantly telling Him that He had the wrong girl. I was grasping, and it became a near-obsession.

According to many psychologists, an excessive need to control others and situations stems from fear. A fear of not getting our needs met. A fear of being rejected. A fear of not being loved.

In marriage, those of us with a propensity to control often dictate to our husbands which gifts we want, which romantic gestures are necessary, how to clean the house and how he should behave in front of friends and family. We may pretend we're just good communicators, but we're actually deeply fearful of being disappointed and having to experience negative feelings and doubts about the security of our marriage.

This need to control often extends to other relationships, including friends, colleagues and even the doctors and therapists who are trying to help us.

And then there are the desperate attempts to control our fertility.

Our overbearing urge to control leaves little room for God. Thankfully, God will never withdraw from us, which can happen in our human relationships. But these controlling behaviors don't leave room for Him to be present or invite Him to reveal His will and plans for us.

> *Our overbearing urge to control leaves little room for God.*

Does this mean we should stop tracking every bodily change or pause treatments? No, but we should adjust our attitude of heart and approach treatment without fear of the unknown. Instead, "Trust in the Lord with all your heart, on your own intelligence do not rely…" (Prv 3:5). While it's good to be diligent in your family building journey, and to discern treatment options and suggestions for conceiving, in the end, we're called to place our total trust in God. Only if we peacefully leave our desire at the foot of the cross do we allow God to do with our efforts what He wills.

In those moments when the false idea of control has me in such a strong grip and even a frenzy, I find it wise to set myself apart, go to quiet prayer and reflection and ask God to show me where control, grasping and demands are separating me from Him. I ask Him to increase my trust in Him and bring me peace, knowing I've prayerfully chosen the efforts to try to conceive.

Let us only attempt to control our surrender, as we bring ourselves to the foot of the cross, as many times as it takes, to be reminded that He's in control.

Reflections

1. When in your infertility struggle have you tried to control your family building journey? How did you feel when you weren't successful in achieving the outcome you desired?

2. In what other situations have you been frustrated about your lack of control? What coping mechanisms were helpful? Could you apply them to your struggle with infertility?

3. Reflect on 2 Corinthians 1:9-10. Personalize the ninth verse, replacing "the sentence of death" with "the loss of control of my fertility" and "God who raises the dead" with "God who makes the barren fruitful." Read it now as, "Indeed, I accept within myself the loss of control of my fertility, that I might trust not in myself but in God who makes the barren fruitful." Meditate on this and consider journaling your thoughts and feelings. Maybe it becomes a prayer mantra. Consider what St. Paul is encouraging when he asks us to place our trust in God and not so much on "man," or ourselves.

Week 2: Prayers Seeking Freedom from Waves of Egotism

DAY 10

From the temptation to feel hurt when my loved ones fail to ask about my infertility struggle, deliver me, Lord…

I'm a verbal processor, and have been for as long as I can remember. I'm sure I got this from my mother. We both like to talk about the details of any given situation and bounce ideas off others. I even have a hard time shopping alone because I simply think and process better when I have someone with whom to think things through.

I need that same dialogue when dealing with the ups and downs, many unknowns and countless deliberations inherent to infertility.

My husband and I didn't tell our loved ones we were struggling to conceive until we'd been trying for six months. I was about to undergo a laparoscopy to determine if I had endometriosis, the diagnosis most consistent with my symptoms and family history. Since I'd be under general anesthesia, we thought our families should know. By the time the surgery came and went, we also told our closest friends and asked everyone for their prayers.

As time progressed, and we still were unable to achieve pregnancy, the intensity and confusion of my emotions made me feel like I was exploding. Internalizing it all was so difficult, and I ached to express what I was feeling. The verbal processor in me longed to talk about it all, so I could think through our situation and find comfort at the same time.

Family and friends' requests for updates seemed far and few between, and I was hurt that they didn't ask more often. I felt like they didn't care about what was turning out to be a real crisis in my life.

To make matters worse, I was surrounded by loved ones who were either pregnant or had small children, and our conversations often revolved around motherhood. I felt like the big elephant in the room. As they shared their experiences on childrearing or pregnancy, I'd quietly stand back, listening. Sometimes it felt like they'd forgotten I was even there. I intentionally made an effort to be interested in and supportive of their lives—after all, I longed for them to be supportive and interested in mine. But sometimes it became too much to handle. I'd shift in my seat or try to give off subtle body language hints, hoping someone might veer the conversation in another direction, or politely excuse myself to find something else to do or someone else with whom to talk.

Despite the significant pain these situations bring, I know deep down that my loved ones care about me and my husband, and any apparent lack of concern is them not knowing how to love me the way I need to be loved. Despite feeling rejected or simply looked over, I have to trust that my friends are wishing the infertility would go away, not me.

> *Despite feeling rejected or simply looked over, I have to trust that my friends are wishing the infertility would go away, not me.*

Infertility does ruin a party! It's a taboo subject that's easier to ignore rather than discuss—even in ministry. Addressing the suffering of others is difficult enough, but infertility adds in the awkwardness of being forced to discuss physical, emotional and sexual intimacy. Loved ones oftentimes choose to leave infertility outside the boundaries of the relationship. If they do know what to say, they may be unsure if you're in the right place, physically or emotionally, to talk about it. Sometimes, when I'm barely holding it together, I don't want the mention of my struggles to burst the very fragile bubble surrounding my heart. Knowing this, loved ones tread carefully. As a result, we feel as though others simply don't care and that we're alone in our struggle.

The most logical solution is to talk to our spouse instead. My husband and I do talk about it all—trust me—but I don't want the burden of infertility to consume our relationship. I also want us to talk about the joys of our marriage, although this can sometimes seem impossible when so much concerning infertility is bursting to get out.

After 15 months of trying to conceive, I sought out a therapist. After visiting with two, I truly connected with a third. She's been a real gift in my life. Not only do I have an outlet for my need to verbally process, but she, too, suffered from infertility and so can easily relate to my experiences and feelings.

My therapist encouraged me to tell my friends and family that I'd like to talk about my infertility, not only to help me process but also to affirm that they care about our struggle. She also told me that I needed to help them know how to help me. The coping experience of infertility isn't too different from that of a cancer patient or someone grieving the loss of a loved one. We're all hurting. Our loved ones try to help us and be there for us, but unless we tell them what we need, they can only guess. Sometimes, people just need it spelled out for them, and there's nothing wrong with that.

I asked my friends if I could send them regular prayer requests and updates. This allowed them to know where we were on the journey and, in turn, they felt more comfortable offering encouragement about specific events or treatment options. They also knew when to celebrate any victories.

For my family members, I flat out told them that I needed to talk about it with them. A couple of my husband's sisters-in-law responded with such love, in that both of them would occasionally pray over me. Being prayed over is such a humbling experience. Every time they offered up words to our Lord aloud for me, I was consumed with such peace and thanksgiving for these wonderful women and holy witnesses in my life.

While these conversations with family and friends have helped tremendously, sometimes you do need to talk to someone who's on the same path. But after I was diagnosed with endometriosis and other hormonal issues affecting my fertility, we couldn't find many other couples struggling with infertility. This call to meet my own dire need extended to other couples in our situation, and led me to co-found Sarah's Hope & Abraham's Promise. Soon after, I left my full-time job at a Catholic parish. Now, when people ask me what I do for a living, I share about my ministry for couples struggling with infertility and pregnancy loss as well as adoptive families.

As I've become more open and forthright about this experience, our loved ones have become more comfortable asking about and being present for us on our journey. Once again, taking the focus off of myself has ultimately brought me peace. Having compassion for how difficult this journey also is for my loved ones, and giving a voice to others through Sarah's Hope & Abraham's Promise, has offered me an outlet for my own voice and allowed it to grow even stronger.

I leave you today with these words from St. Paul:

"Blessed be the God and Father of our Lord Jesus Christ, the Father of compassion and God of all encouragement, who encourages us in our every affliction, so that we may be able to encourage those who are in any affliction with the encouragement with which we ourselves are encouraged by God" (2 Cor. 1:3-5).

Reflections

1. What are your feelings about sharing your infertility experience with loved ones? Have you had to either tell them you'd like to talk about it or set boundaries about what you'd prefer not to discuss? How did they respond?

2. How can you help your loved ones overcome their discomfort about discussing children, fertility, infertility and pregnancies with you or around you?

3. Have you considered visiting with a therapist or licensed professional counselor to discuss your infertility experience and its effects on your life? If you have tried therapy, have you found it helpful? Why or why not?

4. Has the experience of infertility opened your eyes to the pain of others? Do you notice yourself asking about their hardships, or how you can be a good friend during their trials?

Week 2: Prayers Seeking Freedom from Waves of Egotism

DAY 11

From the temptation to feel excluded when I'm not invited to child-centered events, deliver me, Lord…

Sometimes, I feel sorry for my loved ones. They're "damned if they do and damned if they don't" when it comes to inviting the infertile couple to child-centered activities. When we're included, the experience of being surrounded by children and parents often overwhelms us with sadness, grief and loneliness. However, being excluded is a hurtful reminder that we're still without children. Either way, our pain surfaces because we're not part of the in-crowd.

More than once, I've been with a group of friends when someone announced a pregnancy. Those with children congratulated them with, "Welcome to the club!" The club? That definitely felt like a punch to the gut. Not only was our absence of a child a loss, but so was being reminded that I didn't have what it took to be a part of the highly desirable parents' club.

When loved ones don't invite us to children's birthday parties, sporting events or even sacramental occasions like Baptisms, I realize that, oftentimes, they honestly aren't thinking about it or sincerely believe they're helping me avoid a painful situation. But in the moment, when my emotions are further unraveled from crazy medication-induced hormones, it's easy to dismiss even the best of intentions.

While we might not want to attend every single child-focused event, we appreciate having the option in case we're having a good day. After all, we want to be a part of our loved ones' lives and what's nearest and dearest to them, including the milestones of their children. Once I was able see their dilemma, I expressed my feelings. It went something like: "I know it's not always easy to read me and how I feel about being a part of children-centered activities, but I want you to know that, while I might not be up for coming to every event, I'd really enjoy coming to a few. I really do want to be a part of your children's lives, so feel free to include me the next time something pops up. And tell our friends, too."

The response was positive—they appreciated my straight-forwardness and not having to guess my wishes. If this direct approach is too difficult, telling one trusted family member and asking him or her to relay the message serves the same purpose.

Of course, even having laid it all out there, there are times when my loved ones still exclude me or let me down, and I get hurt. In these instances, I remind myself that I'm loved and I'm not alone. I focus on God and His current plan for me. He has a place for me in His club, and that's where my focus needs to be.

Reflections

1. How do you feel about attending children's events? Are your loved ones aware of your feelings? If not, consider telling a few close loved ones and asking them to share with others when appropriate.

2. Child-focused events can be triggers that bring up emotion in your struggle with infertility. Can you think of any other triggers that bring awareness to your suffering? Are these also issues you need to share your feelings about to your loved ones? Are they issues about which you need to pray to further discern the best way to handle them?

3. Can you recall a time when someone around you caused unintentional grief by saying something like, "Welcome to the club!"? How did you react, if at all? What kind of standards do you think are reasonable to hold your loved ones to for comments like this? Would it be fair to talk about it with them, perhaps at a time when you're not feeling triggered or emotional?

Week 2: Prayers Seeking Freedom from Waves of Egotism

DAY 12

From the temptation to make the pregnancies of others about my not being pregnant, deliver me, Lord…

It's easy to feel that the fertile world is out to get you or, at the very least, constantly remind you that you're neither pregnant nor a parent.

After one particular evening with friends, I expressed my frustrations to my husband. "Every time she rubs her growing belly or he talks about building the crib, they're pointing out things I can't relate to," I said. "They're making me feel so awkward!"

Throughout her pregnancy, one particular friend of mine enjoyed wearing fitted clothing that accentuated her growing belly. As the months wore on, she was always rubbing her belly, undoubtedly to soothe the baby if he was being especially active or to relieve her own discomfort. In any case, I couldn't stand it. During every conversation, she'd just sit there, continually rubbing her very pregnant belly, and I began to feel as if she was at worst intentionally reminding me of my pain, or was at best completely oblivious to my suffering of being unable to feel life growing within my body. I resented her.

Deep down, I knew my friend wasn't doing this to offend me. I'm sure if I'd brought attention to her belly rubbing, she would've, rightfully, become upset about my self-centeredness and lack of sensitivity toward her physical discomfort. But on the surface, it felt like a slap in the face.

While suffering with infertility, you'll inevitably be invited to a pregnant friend's baby shower. Her husband will joke about his unease during childbirth classes. She'll eagerly discuss nursery colors and themes with anyone who'll listen. Every conversation will center around pregnancy and children. I don't know what happens, but once a woman sees a positive on a pregnancy test, she temporarily loses the ability to talk about anything else.

As I've mentioned in the other reflections on the spirit of selfishness this week, being in a relationship with others requires times when their needs are placed above our own, even if it forces us to confront the pains of our own suffering.

Friendship is special, and true friendship is rare. At some point, I realized that I didn't want infertility to rob me of my friends as well. I had to relearn how to be a good friend. Not only would I sincerely try to listen with love and compassion to their pregnancy stories but sometimes, on good days, I'd initiate the conversation and ask about their pregnancies. This certainly put them at ease, and they were glad to have permission to speak freely with me about what their hearts were so eager to express. I found friendships could still flourish, despite infertility.

This doesn't mean I was always a perfect friend. I still had to know my boundaries about how much of those conversations I could peacefully handle. I still had to ask for forgiveness from my friends, and of myself, for those probably too frequent times I couldn't stand it anymore and reacted less than charitably. However, the more I attempted to be present for my friends, not only did it get easier, but they were more comfortable being present for me.

Every day, I have to remember that friends being blessed with the gift of pregnancy has nothing to do with my personal journey to parenthood. Our journeys are different. Our stories will be different, and rather than comparing them, I pray for the grace and courage to allow mine to be its own beautiful story. In fact, I've come to realize that my story has the power to be one of great hope and extraordinary love because of my sacrifice, not despite it. Making my story worthy of this description is now my focus.

Reflections

1. Can you recall a time when you struggled with making another woman's pregnancy more about yourself and your struggle with infertility than about celebrating the gift she'd been given? What were the circumstances surrounding that moment, and why do you think you felt that way?

2. Can you recall a time when you felt someone was stealing your thunder, shifting attention to themselves when you were trying to celebrate a blessing or achievement? Was it warranted? How did it make you feel?

3. What practices could you develop to handle negative feelings that creep up when someone begins talking, perhaps at length, about their pregnancy? What are some gracious strategies you might use to remove yourself from the situation or express your feelings?

Week 2: Prayers Seeking Freedom from Waves of Egotism

DAY 13

From the temptation to display poor body languag around others who have been blessed with children, deliver me, Lord...

Oh! Life would be so much easier if I were able to hide my feelings just a little bit. My parents, my friends, even my boss have told me that my facial expressions clearly tell the world what's going on in my head.

When it comes to uncomfortable situations around parents of young children, I've proven I'm incapable of putting on a poker face, smiling on the outside when my emotions are overwhelming me on the inside.

With infertility, feelings are confusing. Attempting to define exactly what I'm experiencing is hard enough, but also having to hide those feelings or pretend they don't exist is nearly impossible. It definitely takes practice. I found it helpful to ask someone to hold me accountable and call me out—quietly, and preferably at a later time when it's just the two of us—whenever I slip and wear my negative feelings on my face. Many times, it's unintentional, and I don't even realize I'm doing it. I'd venture to say mastering being aware of and controlling my body language is a worthy endeavor, as many of life's struggles require us to "keep moving forward" and maintain a pleasing, Christian public persona. This skill will transfer to other uncomfortable situations throughout my life, long after the ache of infertility plagues me.

Being involved in Sarah's Hope & Abraham's Promise has surrounded me with women who understand my situation and serve as accountability and prayer partners. I pray that more and more Sarah's Hope & Abraham's Promise local chapters become a reality to offer this same support for women throughout the world.

Even when it feels like God is holding me down by not alleviating my infertility, I know He will give me the grace to not only survive, but also to thrive. Although the burden of infertility weighs me down, it provides opportunities to grow and be transformed. Learning to be present for others, even when I may not want to be, is a practice of growing in love. While difficult at times, this is a holy experience that helps me grow in virtue.

Reflections

1. Have you had difficulty controlling your body language, especially during conversations revolving around fertility and parenting? Have you considered what your body language or attitude may be conveying?

2. Reflect on 1 Peter 3:8: "Finally, all of you, be of one mind, sympathetic, loving toward one another, compassionate, humble." How does this apply to showing our emotions and feelings through our bodies? What might help you recall this Scripture passage when you're faced with an upsetting conversation?

3. When you find yourself in a displeasing situation, how can you respond in a healthy and loving way?

Week 2: Prayers Seeking Freedom from Waves of Egotism

DAY 14

From the temptation to dismiss the struggles of others as trivial compared to my own, deliver me, Lord...

The burden, shame and guilt of infertility have often defeated me during my family building journey. These heavy feelings have caused me to stumble time and again, focus on licking my own wounds and, often, put blinders up to the struggles of those around me.

At times when I've tried to listen to the suffering others carry, I've found myself comparing it to my grief from infertility. Aside from instances like the death of a loved one, a terminal illness diagnosis or marital struggles, I've often had difficulty offering genuine compassion for their suffering as I wrestled the temptation to think their trials were less of a hardship than mine.

My own suffering felt so overlooked and misunderstood that my heart tried building a protective wall around itself. But by focusing inward rather than outward, I neglected the heartache of others. I became unable to place myself in the shoes of loved ones and see how burdensome their crosses had become.

In his Letter to the Galatians, St. Paul asks us to, "Bear one another's burdens, and so you will fulfill the law of Christ" (Gal 6:2). He doesn't say, "Bear one another's burdens only if you think their suffering is legitimate or their trials are worthy of your attention."

> *[St. Paul] doesn't say, "Bear one another's burdens only if you think their suffering is legitimate or their trials are worthy of your attention."*

We must be careful about judging the struggles of others as insignificant, especially if it's apparent that they're having a difficult time carrying their crosses. We're all called to be like Christ, to serve as His very hands and feet to others in need. This vocation to grow in holiness still applies when we're in the midst of our own suffering.

Answering the call to serve others can be overwhelming when we hardly feel like we're taking care of ourselves. However, I have found refocusing my attention toward someone else often relieves some of my own anxiety, even if it only serves as a distraction at first. I try to see the struggles of my loved ones from their own eyes and look for ways to offer them validation, prayers and support. Ironically, valuing their cries of pain renews my strength for bearing my own suffering as well.

Reflections

1. Have you struggled with taking seriously the burdens and sufferings of others? If so, why have you been tempted to dismiss their trials? Do you need to make any reparations?

2. What would help you to feel more understood and validated in your own suffering from infertility?

3. Pope Francis once said about compassion, "Compassion allows you to see reality; compassion is like the lens of the heart: it allows us to take in and understand the true dimensions. In the Gospels, Jesus is often moved by compassion. And compassion is also the language of God…It is when compassion takes hold, we get involved in the problems of others."[5]

4. How can you become more aware of your capacity for compassion toward others and, at the same time, increase in that compassion? As a starting point, consider reviewing both the Corporal Works of Mercy (feed the hungry, shelter the homeless, clothe the naked, visit the sick and imprisoned, bury the dead and give alms to the poor) and the Spiritual Works of Mercy (counseling the doubtful, instructing the ignorant, admonishing the sinner, comforting the sorrowful, forgiving injuries, bearing wrongs patiently and praying for the living and the dead).

---

[5] Pope Francis (homily during Mass in the Casa Santa Marta, Sept. 17, 2019).

Closing Week 2 with *Graciousness*

Lord, I know this isn't personal. Yes, it's personal in that it's devastating to me. However, the insensitivities of my friends or the joyful lives of my loved ones aren't meant to hurt me personally. I ask You to help me focus less on my own pain and more on You and the beauty You have already put in my life. Help me surrender this focus on my own ego.

Deliver me.

Whenever I am full of my own ego, instead fill me with Your graciousness. Help me to be gracious even when others seem to have forgotten me or my personal struggles. Help me to be gracious at the joys of my loved ones. And Lord, especially help me to be gracious to myself for the times I fail at this task. I pray that when my thoughts turn "self-"centered, that You use them to transform me rather than focus on my own self-pity.

Lord, I am letting go. My selfishness is dissolving, and my graciousness is materializing. Be near me and bless me.

Amen.

WEEK 3

Prayers Seeking Freedom from Waves of Contempt

From Envy to Contentment

When we feel contempt for someone, we've decided they're beneath us, not worthy of our consideration, and we show little regard for them, their story or their feelings. Unfortunately, as we suffer through infertility, it's easy to fall prey to patterns of behavior and attitudes that relay feelings of disgust and anger toward others.

We have this good and beautiful desire for children that appears to be granted so easily to everyone but us, including people who aren't even trying to get pregnant. This often allows jealousy and contempt to have easy access to our hearts.

The prayers this week address the temptations that entertain those negative thoughts and behaviors toward others, which we allow when anger and even jealously get the better of us. Meditate upon them and consider if you've struggled with these temptations. If they aren't specifically what haunts you, pray for those of us who do struggle with them and consider other ways you might need to be freed from having contempt for others in your infertility journey.

Week 3: Prayers Seeking Freedom from Waves of Contempt

DAY 15

From the spirit of envy, deliver me, Lord...

Envy is such an ugly sin against love, and it's the sin I've struggled with most often on this journey. I'm not alone; during our first Sarah's Hope & Abraham's Promise infertility retreat, female attendees named envy as the No. 1 emotion they felt.

Most of my loved ones have been blessed with the gift of new life in their marriages—several of them, multiple times. The envy I feel when I'm around their growing families has been one of the most challenging aspects of my infertility. I've caught myself seeing their blessings as my curses, and putting on a happy face has been, at times, unbearable. Every baby shower, every family gathering where children are present, every time someone announces their pregnancy—you name it, if kids are involved, I have wrestled with jealousy.

Since this sin has been my greatest struggle throughout my infertility journey, I believe God has given me abundant opportunities to overcome it. During gatherings with friends, moments not involving pregnancy announcements or stories of life with small children are far and few between. Perhaps with every opportunity to practice love or generosity of spirit instead of envy, God is asking me to grow in strength to resist the temptation to covet what others have or experience.

I know God desires to deliver me from envy, and that only I keep accepting its presence. Envy might seem to be an emotion we can't control—it's either present or it isn't—and that's partially true. However, I've found a few strategies that have helped lessen its sting or influence.

First, I try to remember to ask for deliverance whenever I feel envy surfacing or I'm tempted to mumble a negative thought during a pregnancy announcement. This has become easier with time. I simply say, "Deliver me, Lord. I no longer want to be jealous."

Second, I pray for the grace to increase my gratitude for the gifts given to others—and then for even more grace to be able to celebrate their gifts. "Lord, fill me with Your grace. Help me find joy in my friends' joys," I say.

And third, I pray for the people I envy. Since I started doing this, I've found that my heart eventually softens toward them, and I no longer feel threatened by their presence.

> "Lord, fill me with Your grace. Help me find joy in my friends' joys."

Ultimately, letting go of jealousy has been integral to my healing. Jealousy has a way of holding us back, of making us feel "less than," which inhibits us from reaching our potential. Jealousy takes so much more from us than infertility does. So, "Deliver me. Fill me with Your grace. And bless them."

As we learn in the epistle of James, *"Blessed is the man who perseveres in temptation, for when he has been proved he will receive the crown of life that [the Lord] promised to those who love him" (Jas 1:12).*

Reflections

1. Have you experienced the temptation to envy the family building journeys of others? To grow in jealousy of their seemingly easy experience of conceiving, being pregnant, going through childbirth, nursing, raising children? In what other ways?

2. How does being tempted toward envy while bearing this cross of infertility make you feel?

3. What are some ideas to help you overcome this temptation to envy?

4. Is there anything you can do to prepare yourself for situations when loved ones make a pregnancy announcement or when conversations about raising small children grow long?

5. We all have a cross, or several crosses, to bear. Consider the crosses of your loved ones who don't struggle with infertility. While fertility may seem to have come easily for them, remember that they bear their share of hardship, too. Offer up prayers for them and their struggles, whether or not you know what they are.

Week 3: Prayers Seeking Freedom from Waves of Contempt

DAY 16

From the resentment I feel toward others who don't struggle with infertility, deliver me, Lord...

"You don't know how this feels."
"You have no idea what you're talking about."
"You don't appreciate how lucky you are to be able to get pregnant."
"I don't want to hear about your burden of fertility and how 'hard' it is for you to avoid pregnancy."

These are a few of the thoughts that have gone through my head in the last decade as I've struggled with infertility. It's been difficult to prevent resentment from entering my heart toward those who not only have what I desire—the gift of fertility—but who also appear to achieve pregnancy so effortlessly. I've found softening my heart toward them even harder if they make ungrateful comments about, or express frustration over, their fertility. I'm ashamed to make such a confession, but it's true.

One clear example in the Bible of resentment over fertility can be found in the Book of Genesis. Sarai and Abram, who would later be renamed Sarah and Abraham, were unable to conceive. The custom of the culture at the time allowed for an infertile woman to provide a mistress to her husband to produce an heir, so Sarai gave her maidservant, Hagar, over to Abram. When Hagar quickly became pregnant, she looked down upon Sarai, since at that time, infertility was often blamed on the wife and considered shameful. Feeling judged, Sarai became outraged and resentful of Hagar's fertility and behavior following the pregnancy. Sarai lashed out at Hagar so much that Hagar ran away with fear (Gn 16:1-6).

For those of us who struggle to conceive, Sarai's resentment at Hagar is easy to understand. (Praise God that today's customs don't include wives having to provide their husbands with fertile women to produce heirs for the family!) We can feel Sarai's resentment—at her own infertility, at the expectation to allow another woman without fertility issues to lay with her husband, at the apparently easy conception Hagar was able to achieve, and at the judgment the mistress placed on her.

It all sounds pretty awful to me.

In our own infertility journeys, we must be prudently aware of those times when we feel resentment toward others creeping in. While we may not be able to control the feeling of resentment itself, we can certainly control what we do with that feeling. Do we act out like Sarai and seek to punish those whom we perceive take their fertility for granted? Do we sever our relationship with them, speak ill of them behind their backs or unabashedly make cruel or thoughtless comments to them? Or do we choose to turn that resentment into prayer—for them and for us?

To lay those feelings at the foot of the cross allows God to use them for our good, for our salvation or even for the salvation of others.

May God deliver each of us from the stain of resentment, and may we increase in our love for others.

Reflections

1. Have you ever felt resentment toward others who don't suffer from infertility? Have these feelings ever caused you to act out like Sarai did toward Hagar? How? Do you need to seek reconciliation with anyone and ask for forgiveness?

2. Reflect on the Beatitudes from Matthew 5:3-12, paying special attention to and meditating on what it means in the eighth verse to have a clean heart: "Blessed are the clean of heart, for they will see God." How can you

make your heart more clean for God, more ready to rid yourself of bitterness and resentment? How will purifying your heart toward others make you more able to see God and draw closer to Him?

3. In his Angelus on May 28, 1989, St. John Paul II spoke about piety, one of the seven gifts of the Holy Spirit.

> *"With [piety], the Spirit heals our hearts of every form of hardness, and opens them to tenderness towards God and our brothers and sisters…The gift of piety further extinguishes in the heart those fires of tension and division which are bitterness, anger and impatience, and nourishes feelings of understanding, tolerance, and pardon. Such a gift is, therefore, at the root of that new human community which is based on the civilization of love. Let us ask the Holy Spirit for a renewed outpouring of this gift, entrusting our prayer to the intercession of Mary, sublime model of fervent prayer and maternal tenderness. May she… teach us to adore God 'in spirit and truth' (Jn 4:23) and to open ourselves with meek and receptive hearts to all who are her children, and therefore our brothers and sisters."* [6]

Reflect on this gift of the Holy Spirit, piety. Consider asking the Lord to help you grow in piety as well, so that you might be given this "new capacity for love of the [others]."

---

6 St. John Paul II. "Angelus." May 28, 1989. *www.vatican.va/content/john-paul-ii/es/angelus/1989/documents/hf_jp-ii_ang_19890528.html*

Week 3: Prayers Seeking Freedom from Waves of Contempt

DAY 17

From the temptation to silently scoff at those who speak of timing their pregnancies at their convenience, deliver me, Lord...

Over the years, I have laughed to myself when engaged or newly married couples, or even well-seasoned married couples, have talked about when they "plan" to have children. Teachers have told me about ideally synching becoming a mother with the school year, banking on conceiving during whichever month fits best with their schedule. Others shared their dreams of traveling during their first year of marriage, after which they'll start popping out kids.

Hmm. Interesting. I've cynically wondered if they've consulted God in these master plans, or if everything in their lives to this point has gone according to plan.

When I was young, I always thought my life would mirror my parents': meet my spouse and get engaged in college, wed six months after graduation and start having children two years later. That was my plan. That was the life I grew up around, the life experience most known to me.

So, it was a rude awakening when my college boyfriend broke up with me immediately following graduation, and my grand plan to begin my adult life by marrying him abruptly dissolved.

That was when I first realized that God didn't necessarily agree that my plan was best for me. In hindsight, it was a blessing. Praise be to God that He knows me better than I know myself, and He was leading me closer to Mark, the amazing man I now call my husband.

But then came infertility, another devastating reminder that God's ways are not my ways.

I try to not let disdain get the better of me when friends mention their big plans of relatively uncontrollable outcomes, such as when they expect to become parents. After all, the majority of couples who desire to conceive actually do so within a reasonable amount of time. Instead, when loved ones talk about their family planning, I try to pray for them, and for God to grant their hearts' desires of parenthood in His perfect timing.

Of course, this could once again bring about my contempt and jealousy. Because…what if? What if it actually comes true for them, while it didn't for me? When it comes to anyone else's fertility, I find acting selflessly is difficult. I have to remind myself that God has His own plans for me—plans for a future full of hope—and that my journey is my own, and no one else's. I pray for God to increase my desire to be encouraging so, in a world full of fear and doubt, I may be a positive voice in the lives of my loved ones. And as I have prayed for their blessings, my own heart has discovered peace on this journey.

Reflections

1. Have thoughts of disdain led you to scoff at the hopes of another who spoke of family planning? Think back to when you were first married and when you hoped to begin growing your family. How would you have felt if someone, jaded by their own suffering, had discouraged and dashed those hopes?

2. Reflect on 1 Thessalonians 5:11, 14-15. How could you encourage others who hope to build their families?

3. Consider how you can practice growing in virtue when someone speaks about their plans to grow their family. How will you overcome the temptation to be uncharitable or discouraging toward your neighbor?

Week 3: Prayers Seeking Freedom from Waves of Contempt

DAY 18

From the temptation to discourage those who speak of their ideal plan to grow their family, deliver me, Lord...

Yesterday, I mentioned thoughts I've experienced when a friend expresses her perfect agenda for family planning. Unfortunately, these thoughts have often found their way into my behaviors as well.

I'm embarrassed to admit that I've displayed poor body language—rolling my eyes or even laughing out loud—when loved ones have spoken of their family building plans, which is hardly charitable. How unloving was I when I succumbed to such temptation, actually choosing to tell them exactly what I thought of their hopes and dreams for how and when they'll become parents?

Throughout my infertility journey, I've had to learn the importance of not letting my hurt and suffering leave me raw, pessimistic and without love or compassion. I can't expect to be considered a true friend if I can't listen and react with love and encouragement to the hopes and dreams of my friends.

God allows us to experience painful life situations because they often draw us the closest to Him. Those experiences shape us into the person He's calling us to become—people full of compassion, mercy, love and forgiveness. We must allow these life experiences to transform how we interact with others. For those of us who have suffered from infertility, this means encouraging not only those who are in the same situation but also encouraging and affirming those who don't struggle with fertility issues. We're called to a higher form of love in finding joy in the positive experiences of our loved ones who have blessings we so ardently desire, like the gift of children.

Whenever I feel a spark of negativity over someone's plans to conceive in such-and-such a time, I remember this call to love.

I pray I don't allow jealousy to guide my response to their holy desires. I pray for true and equal friendship, where I can be present for and celebrate with others and they, in return, may be present for and celebrate with me!

Reflections

1. Can you recall a time when you said something discouraging or negative to a loved one who mentioned their plans of family building? If so, how did they respond?

2. Does taking away the hopes of others or discouraging them heal your infertility? St. Paul says, "Let us then pursue what leads to peace and to building up one another" (Rom 14:19). Reflect on how you might build up another who shares their hopes and dreams of building their family.

3. Oftentimes, acting uncharitably feels like a release in that moment, but then guilt usually creeps into our conscience and we realize our poor behavior. Thankfully, the Sacrament of Reconciliation allows us to confess our wrongdoings or ways we might have hurt others and, therefore, God. When was the last time you received this gift of forgiveness and healing? If it's been a while, I encourage you to go to confession as soon as possible and receive relief and grace from this beautiful sacrament.

Week 3: Prayers Seeking Freedom from Waves of Contempt

DAY 19

From the temptation to react poorly when someone announces a pregnancy, deliver me, Lord...

The second reading at our nuptial Mass included the verse, "Rejoice with those who rejoice, weep with those who weep" (Rom 12:15). If only I'd known the practice I'd have just a year later when we started trying to conceive.

There's a sharp sting in my heart every time someone announces a pregnancy. This is one of the more difficult aspects of infertility for me. I so desperately want to be happy for my loved ones when they're blessed with the gift of new life, but my heart struggles immensely. I've had to rehearse my reaction in private in an attempt to retrain my facial expressions and body language to have a positive knee-jerk reaction when I hear this news.

I've had some unfortunate experiences of finding out about my friends' pregnancies. I definitely didn't enjoy being in the midst of a large group at one particular bridal shower, feeling everyone staring at me to see how I'd react. Some were in shock that our girlfriend chose to tell me at that moment, in that place. My reaction was pretty emotionless as I managed the usual question-and-answer dance, as I call it, when the unknowing deliver baby-related news. After all of the expected must-ask questions, I found an excuse to leave the conversation and scurry off to find talk not related to babies.

Those of us suffering from infertility work very hard at concealing uncharitable, sometimes shameful reactions when others tell us of their pregnancies, especially if our loved ones speak about how easy or unexpected conceiving was for them.

However, other options are available to us.

Our close friends now know that the best way for me to hear about their pregnancies is to either tell my husband ahead of time, so he can share the news when we're alone, or to tell me personally one-on-one. Hearing the news from my husband allows me to deal with any negative feelings I may be struggling with in my own time, so I can truly be sincere in expressing my joy for the expecting couple when I see them. In the second scenario, I don't have to worry about others watching to see how I'll react. I can just have a pleasant conversation with my pregnant friend and work through my feelings as we talk.

Sharing my pain with friends has also helped significantly. When I was first writing this reflection, my husband had just told me that one of my closest friends was pregnant with her first. I'd been out of town when she ran into him at a mutual friend's birthday party and asked him to let me know. I hadn't contacted her yet, but had my usual "congratulations on being pregnant" greeting card ready and planned to buy a small gift to help celebrate the occasion. Rejoicing with her was substantially easier because she knows my struggle and approached delivering her news in such a gentle way. Since I'd shared my pain with her, she was able to graciously walk with me on my painful journey and support me through conversation and prayer, even when it came to announcing her own pregnancy.

It's been easier to rejoice about the children of friends who have wept with me. I feel like they value my own journey toward parenthood, and their allowing me to be open about my experience makes me more open to hearing about theirs. Pasting a smile on my face and asking others about their family lives is more difficult when conversations with them always seem one-sided, and they never get around to returning the interest in my family life.

It's been easier to rejoice about the children of friends who have wept with me.

Regardless, knowing I struggle in this area more often than not, I need to pray for the grace to acknowledge more quickly the joy in the lives of my loved ones when they share joyful news, such as a pregnancy. I need to look beyond myself and not make their news about my own sadness. I need to rejoice with them, for only in such an act is the Holy Spirit most alive and the love of God most visible. In these moments, we glorify our Lord by praising Him for His goodness and mercy, we witness His faithfulness, and we continue to place our trust in Him.

Reflections

1. How do you feel when you hear yet another pregnancy announcement? Does it matter whether it's a stranger or an acquaintance as opposed to a closer family member or friend?

2. Have you considered how you prefer to hear pregnancy announcements? If not, think about it and consider letting chosen loved ones know so they can share your preference with others as they deem appropriate.

3. Reflect on Romans 12:15: "Rejoice with those who rejoice, weep with those who weep." What meaning does this verse have regarding your struggle with infertility? What could God be speaking to you through this verse?

Week 3: Prayers Seeking Freedom from Waves of Contempt

DAY 20

From the temptation to get frustrated when women who've been blessed with children dwell on their pregnancies or on stories about their children, deliver me, Lord…

It's only natural for mothers to be proud and full of love for their children and to speak of them. We cannot expect these proud mothers to withhold conversation about their children whenever they're around us for fear of offending us. They're with their children, for the most part, day and night, and those moments are their day-to-day experiences. Some mothers might have a hard time participating in a conversation if they don't feel welcome talking about their children. For many of them, their children are probably as all-consuming as infertility can be for those of us with this cross.

But for women struggling from infertility, conversations revolving around children are, more often than not, painful. They often result in hurt feelings, especially when friends who are mothers don't seem to care how their comments might affect you.

From my own experience, I've noticed that I have a tolerance level for hearing about motherhood experiences and children. When it becomes too much for me, I'll usually hint through body language that a change in conversation topic would be welcome, and if those cues aren't recognized, I'll politely excuse myself. My struggle is leaving that conversation with a feeling of peace about my own journey to parenthood, but I'm often instead frustrated and saddened.

During those times, it's helpful to remind myself that my friends aren't purposefully trying to hurt me, and that they have every right to celebrate God's blessings in their lives. Isn't that part of being a good witness of Him? Sharing the Good News of how

He's worked in our lives? The rich blessing of children is certainly part of the Good News! And then I, somewhat begrudgingly, also remind myself that I'd most likely be right there with those mothers should I be given that same blessing.

Significant to this struggle is having a holy perspective and putting myself in their shoes, loving them by putting their needs at least equal, if not above, my own. While healthy boundaries are necessary, it's also important to recognize when I'm placing my own needs above those of others, making my pain more important than their joy. In those times, I'm called to share in their Good News and in praising God for their blessings, and remember He is blessing me through my sacrificial love.

Reflections

1. Can you relate to the struggle of becoming frustrated around friends who only seem to talk about parenthood or their children? How have you handled these situations in the past?

2. How might you constructively handle your frustration or impatience with others and what you perceive as a lack of sensitivity? Could you gently tell them how you're feeling or excuse yourself from the conversation? What if it happens repeatedly?

3. Does struggling with feelings like this make you more sensitive to the struggles of others in areas to which you can't personally relate? Have you reached out to ask how you could be more supportive? Such thoughtfulness, or simply saying you care, may be all you need to do. How would you feel if someone did that for you?

Week 3: Prayers Seeking Freedom from Waves of Contempt

DAY 21

From the temptation to flaunt the freedom my child-free life offers while in the presence of others with children, deliver me, Lord...

In an effort to "support" me, acquaintances and even loved ones have suggested I look on the bright side of living child-free. And certainly, there are benefits to not having children: I can travel at the last minute; I can stay out late at night; my body isn't affected by having a small person growing inside of me. The list goes on.

Focusing on these child-free positives does help lessen the ache of the loss I truly feel, and has been an important strategy in coping with infertility. However, I've been perhaps too focused and intentionally boastful at times when part of me has wanted to make those with children jealous and envious of me for once. In those moments, I've truly been insensitive to parents who have to make special arrangements or who can't participate in extra activities for whatever reason.

My pain doesn't give me a free pass to inflict pain on others, either intentionally or unintentionally. Numerous times, I've had to ask the Lord to guide my tongue and help me filter my thoughts before speaking them. I've adapted as one of my mantras, "Set a guard, Lord, before my mouth, keep watch over the door of my lips" (Ps 141:3). If we desire and even expect others to be sensitive to us and what's going on in our lives, we should do the same for them.

So, yes, I try to celebrate the positives of my life, including those blessings from living child-free. However, these blessings are the ones I try to hold in my heart, keep to myself or, better yet, write in my personal journal of thanksgiving (along with all of the blessings I can think of!). My mother-in-law once gifted me and my husband with a journal for this purpose and it's such a joy to look back through and be reminded of our large and small blessings from God. Whenever I'm feeling frustrated or hopeless, I pick up my journal and read, in my own words, how the Lord has showered me with His love and humbly praise Him.

Reflections

1. It may seem contradictory to ask you to recognize the joy of your current state, then to examine whether you might be too boastful about the benefits of living a child-free life, but there's a fine line that can easily be crossed. Have you ever flaunted this freedom in front of others who might not have the same freedoms as you?

2. Due to jealousy or anger, have you ever intentionally tried to hurt a friend or loved one by bragging about an experience on which they're missing out? Do you need to ask for forgiveness? Reflect on Proverbs 17:27: "Those who spare their words are truly knowledgeable, and those who are discreet are intelligent." How does this apply to you?

Closing Week 3 with Contentment

Lord, I have such contempt for those who haven't had to suffer as I have—for those who have the life I so desire. My contempt tempts me with a feeling of power when I feel out of control. I find I'm unable to feel joy for those with children or hope for their happiness. Help me lift them up. Help me surrender this envy.

Deliver me.

I pray that this contempt doesn't separate me from my friends and family. I ask for the jealousy fueling my contempt to fall away. In its place, please fill me with contentment. I long to feel at peace with and to accept my current circumstances—to no longer worry, to no longer despair, to no longer control, to no longer feel this enormous void. I long to rest from negative, envious thoughts and to soothe my heart and mind with Your calming grace.

Lord, I am letting go. The contempt and envy are washing away, and I am being flooded, instead, with the grace of contentment. Be near me and bless me.

Amen.

WEEK 4
Prayers Seeking Freedom from Waves of Anger
From Anger to Peace

I never knew anger could be so vicious, so all-consuming, so powerful until I experienced infertility. This week speaks to me personally because I've been vengeful, impatient, easily offended, judgmental and obsessive. I've lashed out at my friends, my spouse, my family, my physicians and, more often than not, God. However, as much as releasing a torrent of emotions can feel good in the moment, anger hasn't served me well.

Anger has a unique way of separating us from love. Even if we smile politely and are charitable to others, anger still shows in our body language—in the tension of our mouths, when our smiles don't reach our eyes, in our choice of words. Anger isolates us from friends and loved ones, and especially from God. It's as though a thick stone wall covered in vines of thorns surrounds us, repelling anyone who shows us love or concern.

But we have a right to be angry. I AM angry! I'm angry at this situation and the time I've spent experiencing pain rather than joy.

This is what makes anger even more difficult. It isn't an emotion we can necessarily control, and it has the capacity to destroy our relationships if we let it out in an unhealthy way. But even worse, it can destroy us—and eventually, our relationships—if we repress it inside. It festers and eats away our sense of self, our peace and our happiness.

This week, we attempt to not only destroy the seeds that grow into anger but also release anger without destroying those we love. Week 4 is dedicated to prayers that help soothe the storm.

Week 4: Prayers Seeking Freedom from Waves of Anger

DAY 22

From the spirit of anger, deliver me, Lord...

During my infertility journey, I've directed my feelings of anger everywhere. Sometimes, they've manifested as frustration with my body and what I see as its brokenness—what my body can't do. Other times, I've been angry at what loved ones have said about my cross of infertility, or what they haven't said. I've been angry at someone I care about for no reason other than she had a child and I didn't. I've been angry at doctors (and a pregnancy test) for delivering bad news.

I've been angry at myself for constantly battling feelings of anger—and envy and sadness.

And absolutely, I've been angry at God.

As one of the five stages of the grief process, anger isn't unexpected when dealing with the uncertainty of whether you may ever be able to bear children or have a family. Infertility is a major life crisis! Although for me, this doesn't come close to describing the enormity of the cross of infertility. Feeling angry is natural for someone trapped in this state of unknowns and ups and downs.

Feeling anger, in and of itself, isn't sinful. Jesus even becomes angry with the money changers selling and buying goods in the temple area of Jerusalem (Jn 2:13-17). It's what we do with our anger that matters—if we allow it to affect our attitude toward ourselves and others.

In his letter to the Ephesians, St. Paul says,

"Be angry but do not sin; do not let the sun set on your anger, and do not leave room for the devil...No foul language should come out of your mouths, but only such as is good for needed edification, that it may impart grace to those who hear. And do not grieve the holy Spirit of God, with which you were sealed

for the day of redemption. All bitterness, fury, anger, shouting, and reviling must be removed from you, along with all malice" (Eph 4:26-27, 29-31).

If we allow the spirit of anger to fester and corrupt us, it affects our very nature, influencing our thoughts and even informing our conscience. Ultimately, anger has the ability to change us into someone we don't want to be, and others won't want to be around.

There are strategies for dealing with anger. When anger bubbles up just beneath the surface but hasn't yet erupted, we can give ourselves permission to express it in a healthy way. Maybe we scream at the top of our voices in our own personal spaces, or take a pillow and hit a bed with it over and over again. Perhaps we write a letter to God with as much force and intensity as possible, pressing the pen hard into the paper. I have friends who've alleviated anger through activities like sprinting, kickboxing or dancing, finding physical movement allows them to let go of some of those big feelings. Really, any release can make a difference when anger begins to feel overwhelming, and letting loose in a safe and healthy environment helps keep anger under control during times when it's socially necessary. This release is also important for our well-being, as repressing anger is just as harmful to our emotional and psychological health as erupting anger all over someone else.

When my anger has already spewed out, I do whatever I can to seek God's peace and, sometimes, forgiveness. Figuratively, or literally, if needed, I lay my anger at the foot of the cross of Jesus and ask Him to release me from my anger and fill me with calm. I spend as much time as possible in silent prayer, taking deep breaths and listening to what God has to say to me. God longs to give us His peace, but we need to be still enough, and quiet enough, to receive it.

Opening ourselves to receiving God's peace helps not only in that moment of intensity, but also treats the root of our anger. I've found God has an amazing way of speaking to me during these times that allows my heart to once again see beauty and restores my hope. Oftentimes, He will reveal someone I need to forgive—someone who's hurt me along this journey or long before I even experienced infertility. Sometimes I need to forgive God, Himself.

Forgiveness is key to healing from anger. Anger has a way of building upon itself, and sometimes getting rid of seemingly unrelated anger helps me to deal more peacefully with my current struggle. So, whenever God stirs my heart toward action during these moments when I'm begging for calm, I respond—even if I don't understand. His ways of restoring my peace involve my whole self, not just my infertility!

Reflections

1. Do you struggle with a spirit of anger stemming from your infertility? Have you noticed your temperament changing to bitterness or fury? Has it affected your relationships? Do you need to seek forgiveness from or reconciliation with anyone?

2. Have you ever told God in prayer that you're angry with Him or His ways? How has your anger toward God expressed itself—through blame, unforgiveness, guilt? Ask God to reveal how to address your anger in a healthy way.

3. Prolonged anger can have several detrimental effects on our bodies, such as headaches, stomachaches, dizziness and shakiness, or even chronic sleep disorders and blood pressure issues. It can destroy relationships if you're unwilling to address the problem. Have you noticed mental, physical or relational side effects resulting from a spirit of anger? Should you consider seeking guidance from a spiritual director or a faith-based counselor?

4. When you're quiet in prayer, what anger from your past does God reveal? To whom or to what situations do you feel called to offer forgiveness?

Week 4: Prayers Seeking Freedom from Waves of Anger

DAY 23

From the temptation to obsess over my struggles with infertility, deliver me, Lord...

For those of us with Type A personalities, struggles with conceiving or pregnancy loss undoubtedly make us feel like we're trying to build a house of sticks in the middle of a tornado. Very little is within our control. No matter what I've done, I've never been able to will a pregnancy, force conception or dictate what an eventual pregnancy might look like. Feeling so out of control for a big matter of life like fertility is maddening.

Every 28 days or so, those of us with infertility are disappointed by another failed cycle. We're left wondering what went wrong—what we did wrong, what we failed to do, what we missed. It's easy to become overwhelmed with these circling thoughts and unrelenting disappointment.

I can share how I've personally handled the myriad thoughts, emotions and treatment options that consume my mind. As I mentioned in Week 2, I'm a verbal processor and best understand the world when I'm able to vocalize my thoughts, feelings and ideas. So, one of my coping mechanisms is talking it out. Thinking aloud, bouncing ideas off others and receiving a healthy amount of feedback helps me to discern, understand and see the bigger picture.

What has also helped me tremendously is finding a trusted confidante I can bear my soul to—someone in addition to my spouse—who is impartial. That person has often been a counselor since I realized early on that I didn't want my marriage or friendships to carry the entire burden that comes with infertility. Counseling is a great way to process infertility because a counselor isn't also feeling this pain or expecting friendship in return. I've found it's a safe place for me to discuss my infertility struggle because

I'm allowed to be self-focused on how it affects me emotionally, psychologically and even spiritually.

A warning: Both verbal and internal processors need to be wary of dwelling too much on the cross of infertility. Obsession with worldly desires, including our sufferings, often pulls our eyes away from Christ. I've found discerning when I'm being obsessive to be difficult, since infertility requires so much in terms of organizing, focusing on details and advanced planning. One telltale sign that I'm too "involved" in the struggle to conceive is my anxiety level. What leads us to Christ brings peace. When I feel anxious, I know my eyes, as well as my heart and mind, are focused on the wrong object, and I'm letting infertility define me.

This brings me to my most important point—our infertility doesn't define us. In fact, let me reiterate that—our infertility doesn't define us! We're more than barren wives. We're precious daughters of our Lord, and our own conception, our own existence, was carefully and purposefully crafted. We've all been given unique gifts in order to build the Kingdom of God and to glorify Him.

Sure, this infertility journey may bring us to our knees, sometimes more often than not, but we're more than darkness. We're light, full of hope, promise and possibility. Whenever I feel obsessive thoughts arise, I pray to overcome them, to be able to push them aside so that, once again, I can be full of this light!

> *Counseling is a great way to process infertility because a counselor isn't also feeling this pain or expecting friendship in return.*

Reflections

1. In your struggle with infertility, have you found it helpful to talk with others, such as your spouse, family, friends, counselor, clergy or a support group?

2. What are some ways you've tried to distract yourself from obsessing over this burden of infertility? Think of ideas to store away for when you find yourself growing (too) anxious. Even a mental list of your favorite activities will help take your mind off of your suffering for a short or long while.

3. Consider how your struggle with infertility hinders you from living your best life and from being a light to others. How are you a light in the darkness? Do you feel God may be calling you to uncover your light?

Week 4: Prayers Seeking Freedom from Waves of Anger

DAY 24

From the temptation to complain, deliver me, Lord...

No one wants to suffer alone, and no one should have to, but few people understand the true pain of the cross of infertility. Those of us carrying this cross often feel as though we're suffering alone. We long for a friend who really understands the depths of despair we feel, and who also has the endurance to listen and console us anytime we need to hear a loving voice.

Unfortunately, that's not reality for most of us. Friends who are empathetic and want to be helpful have their own lives, and others, as wonderful as they are, simply aren't capable of comprehending the significance of this cross. Our feelings dismissed, almost always unintentionally, we find ourselves complaining in an attempt to both force others to understand how terrible infertility is and force their compassion. Sometimes, this is out of anger; sometimes, it's a new aspect of our grief; and sometimes, we simply have an overwhelming need for our feelings to be validated.

Similar to the temptation to obsess over our suffering from fertility struggles, there's a fine line between the healthy aspects of sharing our feelings and the destructive effects of complaining. While our loved ones—and our spouses, for that matter—want to be present for us and help us carry this immense burden of infertility, sharing the oftentimes painful experiences of our infertility journey is different than complaining about them.

Of course, we find beauty in becoming vulnerable to those we love through our honesty about the hardships of infertility. This vulnerability is essential to the transformational opportunity inherent in our struggle. But by complaining at every occasion, we become trapped in our negative emotions and are prevented from being receptive to healing. Anger, despair and jealousy have a way of deflecting love so little penetrates our hearts. The absence of this love makes the pain seem so much greater.

We have to try to see our sufferings for what they are and allow the Holy Spirit to work through them to bring us closer to God. If we're too angry or pessimistic and too tempted to complain, we might miss the opportunity to experience the Spirit moving within us.

Over these many years, I've had to figure out how to suffer, and to share, without complaining. Initially, I truly wanted to let out every terrible thought, feeling or injustice I was experiencing. But I soon noticed the weariness on my friends' faces when I would, once again, go on and on and on. So, when I was asked or when sharing was appropriate, I tried to temper my words, the emotion or simply the length of my story. I began by just letting them know the facts of my medical diagnoses, the process of my journey and upcoming procedures and testing. This both shortened the time I spent discussing infertility and helped remove some of the emotion not always appropriate in social settings.

This isn't to say that I repressed my emotions, but I did work at minimizing negative feelings and focusing on the positives. When I struggled to find a positive, I added something along the lines of, "I'm trying to make the most of this and see how God can use this cross to bring me closer to becoming who I'm meant to be." You've heard the expression, "Fake it till you make it." This is what I had to do.

At the beginning, I didn't believe anything beautiful could come from my suffering. But eventually, I saw glimpses of how I'd been transformed and focusing on the positive became easier. This was especially important when I participated in an infertility support group, where it was even more tempting to overly complain, especially with several of us feeding off of each other's negative energy. When this would happen, I'd leave the group more disheartened than when I arrived.

I now encourage infertility support groups to end each session with each person focusing on or sharing something positive that happened because of their struggle or hope they found since the last meeting. Although many will push back because, yes, complaining feels so good, wouldn't we all rather be healed?

Reflections

1. If you honestly examine how you speak about your infertility journey with others, would you say you complain more than you should? Has anyone ever brought this to your attention before, either jokingly or honestly?

2. What do you consider to be the difference between talking about your cross of infertility by stating what's happened and your feelings and just complaining? How do you think others receive what you're saying when you seem to complain and grumble every time your infertility journey comes up?

3. How might you resist the temptation to complain about your suffering? Perhaps read the biography of a saint who might inspire you. One suggestion is St. Catherine of Siena, a doctor of the Church, who, in her book, "Dialogue of St. Catherine of Siena," reveals what Jesus said to her about suffering patiently, without complaining: "Consider that the love of divine charity is so closely joined in the soul with perfect patience, that neither can leave the soul without the other. For this reason (if the soul elect to love Me) she should elect to endure pains for Me in whatever mode or circumstance I may send them to her. Patience cannot be proved in any other way than by suffering, and patience is united with love as has been said."

Week 4: Prayers Seeking Freedom from Waves of Anger

DAY 25

From impatience, deliver me, Lord...

"I want it, and I want it now!"

So, so badly, do I want it now! With infertility, not only are we saddened each month by not becoming pregnant, but we also have the added worry and fear that we're one month closer to the time when conceiving will no longer be possible. Every month that passes moves the hand forward on our biological clock. Living under the illusion of a linear timeline, we grow short of breath in our prayers, as we remind our heavenly Father that we're only getting older, so He better get a move on with our future, lest He forget this predicament He's put us in.

Understandably, impatience can overwhelm our lives. This negative emotion makes us feel as if the rest of our life is on hold. Nothing matters except trying to conceive. We have no life until we have a child!

It's easy to look back and regret not getting married sooner or not trying to conceive sooner, but we can't change the past. Fortunately, God can and does work in all circumstances, even advanced maternal age. Only that makes me ask, "Why doesn't He?" and "Why doesn't He now?"

I doubt any of us will ever completely understand why this cross has been allowed for us. I know I'll never understand why this journey has to be so long and drawn out. But I do know that postponing my life or putting happiness on hold until I become pregnant is truly robbing me of what's in the present moment. God asks us to focus on the here and now. He wants us to consider how He's calling us to be fruitful, how to address our infertility, how to nurture our marriage and how we can be healed. He wants us to be patient with Him and leave the future in His hands. He asks us to become aware of what's right in front of us and let go of our impatience, to stop waiting for what may or may not come our way.

Yes, our biological clocks are ticking, but Mother Nature will not overcome God. Trust this and find peace, at least for today. We can worry tomorrow about the patience we'll need to continue. For today, just remember that we and our future are in God's hands, and His timing is perfect. It always has been.

Reflections

1. How do you handle the anxiety that comes with another day or year passing without having overcome infertility? In your own way or through the comments of others, have you felt the pressures of Mother Nature and your biological clock? How have you responded to any inappropriate comments about your getting older and not yet having children?

2. Reflect on Psalm 40:1-18. How does this "psalm of David" speak to you regarding waiting for God's plans for your family to be revealed?

3. Can you recall another aspect of your life when you had to patiently wait for God's perfect timing? Perhaps it was before you met your spouse or when you were trying to find a job, and you could only do so much to try to achieve what you were hoping for, and the rest was put in God's hands to come to fruition. What would you say to your younger self if you wrote her a letter now? How would you reassure her about the future? Consider writing that letter as a therapeutic exercise then consider what you can take from it to comfort yourself today. If you enjoy this exercise, you may consider imagining what your future self might write to your current self. If you were ever able to conceive, how might future you comfort yourself now? What if you were never able to conceive?

Week 4: Prayers Seeking Freedom from Waves of Anger

DAY 26

From the temptation to be quick to take offense, deliver me, Lord...

We can all be a little too focused on ourselves when we're going through something that's all-consuming, and easily take offense when someone is seemingly insensitive.

"Didn't they know how that would make me feel?" we think.

No, they probably didn't. Very few people consider how everyday topics of conversation might come across as offensive to those struggling with infertility.

Numerous conversations have hit me straight in the gut, and I've had to learn to give people a break and react less sensitively during interactions with others. Yes, people can be inconsiderate but for the most part, they truly mean well and deserve the benefit of the doubt. It must be exhausting for our loved ones to feel like they're always walking on eggshells, always filtering what they say to avoid hitting a nerve with those of us struggling with infertility.

With every interaction, I try to put myself in their shoes and imagine how I'd behave in the same situation if infertility had never entered my world. Would I have talked about the timing of when I hoped to conceive? I most definitely would have—and in fact, I did! Would I be excited to discuss my child's birthday party with my friends? Of course. Many topics of conversation may be difficult to hear but aren't intended to cause me pain. Friends are simply sharing their struggles, dreams and plans. And I want to be the kind of friend who's present for the joys and sorrows of their lives.

Certainly, being present for these normal aspects of friends' lives sometimes causes me sadness, but I've chosen not to add being unnecessarily offended to the burden I carry. Amazingly, this has opened new avenues for my friends and loved ones to help carry my burden as well!

Reflections

1. Have you noticed yourself becoming quick to take offense at behaviors you interpret as insensitive to your struggle with infertility? If so, how have those interactions played out, and do you need to seek forgiveness for any poor behavior you've displayed?

2. Are you open to listening to others when they confide in you about their own struggles or aspirations? Do you have a hard time listening if what they're sharing has to do with family building?

3. Reflect on these passages from Proverbs, "The quick-tempered make fools of themselves..." (14:17a), and James, "Know this, my dear brothers: everyone should be quick to hear, slow to speak, slow to wrath, for the wrath of a man does not accomplish the righteousness of God" (1:19-20). How you can apply these Scriptures to your struggle with being overly sensitive?

Week 4: Prayers Seeking Freedom from Waves of Anger

DAY 27

From the temptation to pursue every solution to infertility the world presents without pause to consider the consequences, deliver me, Lord...

When did you realize your desire to be a mother? Was it as a young girl, playing "house" with your baby dolls? We're all familiar with the scenario: small children pretend to cook in their play kitchen, feeding their dolls, rocking them to sleep, swaying them back and forth and even singing to them so as to soothe their fussy babies. It isn't uncommon for young children who have siblings being nursed by their mother to imitate breastfeeding their baby dolls, copying what mommy does in her role as the family nurturer.

Perhaps you discovered your wish to become a mom when you and your now-husband began to seriously discuss the possibility of marriage and lay out what your hopes and dreams together would be, including having children.

Then upon becoming a newlywed, you likely naturally assumed that having children would come easily, maybe even too easily, so you avoided it for a bit in those early days of marriage so as to establish your relationship together as a husband and wife before you brought children into the picture.

For those of us who later learn that we suffer from infertility, the reality is utterly devastating. Will our delay in sharing in the gift of motherhood be temporary—a few months? Years? Or, dare we even fear that it is a permanent truth?

Every woman's infertility journey looks different. As someone who has lived my own journey for more than a decade, I know what it can feel like to become impatient in the waiting. Desperate even. So many repeated failed attempts. It's disheartening, and sometimes maddening, to have to begin again every month. As the months begin to multiply and turn into years of trying to conceive, it's easy to understand how hope can often fade and we long for the wait to end. What was once an assumption that it wouldn't require any effort, much less become a hardship, the desire to have children morphs for many women into desperation at becoming a mother, being willing to do whatever it takes to make it happen. No woman could ever be blamed.

We live in a time when the world presents many options for family building. In our search to find ways to end our infertility, we're bombarded with potential solutions. There is no shortage of information on options available to us. We are told of old wives' tales, run into options of medical treatment ranging from homeopathic medicine to Natural Procreative Technology to assisted reproductive technology, and then there's adoption, whether it's domestic, international, foster care or adopting an embryo. And everyone has an opinion about what they think we should do. When others find out about our struggle to conceive, they aim to provide hope to us by sharing stories of how others they know finally became pregnant.

I know from experience that the passing of time without a baby in her arms can lead a woman into feeling pressured to take advantage of everything within her reach to make that dream of motherhood come true. In our often overwhelming sense of urgency to end our pain in suffering from infertility, the waiting can easily grow into anger at what's seemingly become our only options to conceive. It isn't fair that while everyone else around us seems to be so easily able to get pregnant, we are only able to join the ranks of motherhood by having to weave through multiple solutions that often leave us feeling stripped, prodded, pressured and sometimes even as though the dignity of us and our future child is being threatened.

While we are incredibly blessed to live in a time that offers a variety of solutions to our infertility, it's important that we also take time to pause and consider our actions before we just move forward with everything the world presents to us.

Every possibility to end our infertility does have consequences—not only the hope of finally become a mother but several of the solutions have significant negative costs that are worthwhile considering before making a decision to pursue. We would be amiss to not take into account how each one could affect not only us as an individual, but also our spouse and future child biologically, mentally and spiritually. We are obligated as children of God to be good stewards of our bodies, remembering and ensuring the respect of our own human dignity.

> ...it's important that we also take time to pause and consider our actions before we just move forward with everything the world presents to us.

Whether it's talking to others who have approached their infertility in a variety of ways, meeting with our priest, spiritual director or a trusted faithful friend, or, at the very least, doing some research into what each option can mean long-term, we would be wise to do our best to fully understand each possibility that would build our family.

As time progresses, so will science and medicine. While we may be tempted to take advantage of every solution to our infertility, let us pray for deliverance from being too rash in our decision making and ask God for the grace to pause instead and consider what each option could mean, both for us and any future child we may have. Ask Him to reveal the real consequences of every option we may consider so that we can make informed decisions and feel good about our path forward.

Reflections

1. In your journey with infertility, have there been times when you have felt the impatience to conceive swell up so much within you that the increasing sense of urgency has led you to pursue every treatment or suggestion offered to you? What have those attempts looked like for you and even for your spouse?

2. When choosing to act on these methods to build your family, have you taken the time to consider all of the ramifications that each solution comes with? From extreme diets to taking exhaustive supplements and pills to side effects associated with various medical treatments, there are real consequences that can not only wreak havoc on your body but can also affect your mental health and fail to consider long-term effects for you and any baby who might result in the effort. Have you and your spouse discussed any negative consequences and even the moral implications associated with each option, and if you both feel as though continuing with the decision upholds the human dignity of each of you and any future child you may have? If no, why not?

3. How does it make you feel to be reminded to pause and consider not only the natural consequences but also the bioethical and moral perspectives of each solution to infertility? Does the idea that some solutions might not be worth pursuing due to either their negative effects or ethical considerations upset you? Consider praying through your feelings by journaling about them if you think it could be helpful to thinking them through.

Week 4: Prayers Seeking Freedom from Waves of Anger

DAY 28

From being quick to judge the decisions of others about the way they pursue, or choose not to pursue, building their family, deliver me, Lord...

> "Which medicines have you tried, Clomid or Femara?"
> "Oh, you've been trying to get pregnant for six months, and you're already pursuing fertility treatments?"
> "Have you seen this other doctor yet?"
> "Have you talked to any adoption agencies?"
> "Have you considered starting the adoption process even if you're still trying to get pregnant?"

These are just a sliver of the questions that arise at any gathering of couples facing infertility. Our choices can seem daunting, from doctors to medications and surgical options to how long to pursue fertility treatments before stopping altogether. As co-founder of Sarah's Hope & Abraham's Promise, I've had more than my fair share of opportunities to recommend the path each person should take. It's very tempting—especially for a verbal processor like me!—to offer, even when unsolicited, advice to others who share their infertility struggle with you.

My intention is usually innocent—I just want to help and let others know when I feel they have a better option. But at times, there can be an accompanying judgment on my part. If I can refrain from speaking the judgment aloud, it's still in my heart. And since the heart has the power to speak, the recipient subconsciously hears this message, staining that relationship indirectly.

Everyone bearing the cross of infertility has their own journey to traverse. What my husband and I discerned as a good treatment option might not be the same for someone else, and that's OK.

I believe we have a duty to help others in forming their conscience about approaches to infertility that don't uphold the dignity of every human life and those that do, like Natural Procreative Technology, or NaProTECHNOLOGY. Many couples suffering from fertility issues aren't aware options exist that respect the marriage covenant as well as the dignity of human life. Recognizing that our advice can sometimes push people further away rather than bring them in, I prayerfully consider whether to share the good news of reproductive healthcare. If I notice any judgmental thoughts in my heart, I remain quiet, knowing this isn't the right time.

When St. Teresa of Calcutta was head of the Missionaries of Charity, she kept a list of ways to cultivate humility for the sisters in her care. Two of her bullet points: "Keep busy with your own affairs and not those of others" and "Do not interfere in the affairs of others." While evaluating the family building decisions of others may be tempting, especially when we feel we have a vast knowledge of all things concerning infertility, we need to remember to turn our gaze back on Jesus and seek His guidance in our own family building journey. We need to spend time praying about our own decisions and not focusing so much on the decisions of others.

This brings me to the beauty of adoption. In the first few years of my infertility journey, when we were discerning material for our infertility support group, I asked that adoption not even be mentioned. I personally wasn't ready to consider adoption as an option yet. The calling to use the path of adoption to build a family is a personal and unique vocation. As I'm sure you've discovered in your own journey, people are quick to suggest adopting a child to those who want to become a parent but have yet to do so biologically.

Not everyone who's unable to conceive is called to adoption. Adoption is its own calling, separate from the inability to have biological children. Again, we're each called to a different path.

Apart from lending a supportive shoulder and listening ear to others suffering from infertility, praying for them and their decisions is best. Ask God to reveal His will for their family and to give them wisdom and discernment as they carry their cross and follow

Him. I absolutely share my journey and the path we've chosen when appropriate or when asked, but always with the disclaimer that this is the path God intended for me! And I always end with, "What do you think God is intending for you?"

Reflections

1. Do you find yourself being quick to judge others in their family building journeys? Has anyone ever shared that you've hurt their feelings because something you said came across as judgmental? Has envy, resentment or anger caused you to think uncharitably about the decisions of others in how they carry their crosses of infertility?

2. One of my favorite prayers is the Litany of Humility by Merry Cardinal del Val, who was secretary of state to St. Pius X. It appeared in the 1963 prayer book for Jesuits, but you may find it in the appendix on page 137. When you read this prayer, take extra time to reflect on lines that speak to you. One line that speaks to me: "From the desire of being consulted, deliver me, O Jesus."

3. Are you distraught over someone else's situation and plagued with a nagging feeling to say something? If so, consider speaking to a spiritual director or clergyman to determine your heart's intention before offering this likely unsolicited counsel. If a loved one is indeed making decisions that you believe are harmful, even spiritually, correction should be expressed in love and with gentleness.

Closing Week 4 with *Peace*

Lord, I'm so angry. I've been resentful and impatient, and I've lashed out at my friends, my family, my spouse, my Church and even You. Help me release my anger. Help me surrender these judgments.

Deliver me.

In whichever thoughts, actions or attitudes that anger is present, Lord, exchange it for peace. I pray that I find healthy ways of letting go of this anger. Give me the courage to forgive those who've disappointed me so I may seek true healing—healing that only comes once forgiveness has left my heart. Help me find acceptance and gratitude for the present moment. Give me serenity.

Lord, I am letting go. My anger is surfacing and venting away as a sense of peace consumes me. Be near me and bless me.

Amen.

WEEK 5

Prayers Seeking Freedom from Waves of Despising God
From a Lack of Faith to Courage

No one wants to admit that they struggle with despising God. How could someone possibly despise God? It must be the sin of all sins, right?

If you can honestly say that you've never been angry with God or irritated with how your life has turned out because of things beyond your control, I'm seriously impressed.

I also don't believe you.

Getting upset with God doesn't make you a bad person. In the Bible, Job cries out to God for making his life a continual hell.

> *"How long before you look away from me and let me alone till I swallow my spit? If I sin, what do I do to you, O watcher of mortals? Why have you made me your target? Why should I be a burden for you?" (Jb 7:19-20).*

Job is pleading with God to just leave him alone. He doesn't understand why he's been given his sufferings and begs for a break. Can't we all relate to Job's lamentation? In those moments, many of us find ourselves exasperated and even frustrated with our God.

This week's prayers address those times when we have difficulty trusting God and instead try to control the situation and fix it. This section is especially for the days we most struggle with cursing God, ingratitude, distrust and impatience. I pray these reflections offer a renewal of faith and the promise of courage to face the hardship of infertility.

Week 5: Prayers Seeking Freedom from Waves of Despising God

DAY 29

From the spirit of faithlessness, deliver me, Lord...

Incredulity, or disbelief, is a grave sin against faith. The Apostle Thomas was famously incredulous when he wouldn't believe Jesus was whom He said He was until seeing the crucifixion scars in Jesus' hands and feet.

We display weakness in faith when we let our disappointment about our infertility overwhelm us. It surfaces when we begin to believe that if God existed, He wouldn't let us suffer the painful reality of being unable to conceive. Infertility affects our faith when we pull away from God because we don't understand how He works. We ponder the age-old question: Why do bad things happen to good people? Our loving God wouldn't allow them, so He must not exist, right? This whole "God thing" must be a fairy tale.

Nothing could be further from the truth.

Our precious Father adores and loves us more than we can possibly comprehend. As long as we walk this earth, we'll never completely understand all of the roads of our life or the circumstances we must endure. Not much can be said other than to accept the beautiful and great mystery that is faith, belief in the unseen. There's no other way to true joy—not in this life, nor in the one to come.

We can try to test God like Thomas did, saying aloud, "God, I won't believe you exist unless you remove this disease of infertility, and we conceive today." If it doesn't happen, do I then refuse to believe that God exists? Or if I still accept He exists, do I add, "but You obviously don't love me"? That's a pretty big pill to swallow. It is for me, anyway.

While God may not directly cause our infertility, He can turn all things into good for those who love Him. Faith means trusting that He will take this burden and create something magnificent with it. We only have to let Him. In this lifetime, we may never know the blessings that have come through our journey of infertility, but that doesn't mean they aren't happening. A friend of a friend of a friend might have a life-changing moment because they heard about what we're enduring.

Everyone has suffering in this life, and infertility is our suffering to bear at this moment. It won't always be this way, though. Even if the infertility is never resolved, there can always be a place of healing and peace. Faith requires it, and I hope for it. Whenever I feel my faith faltering, I simply ask to be filled with Him once again. Feeling His presence inside me has the amazing power to restore my faith.

Reflections

1. Has your experience with infertility caused you to struggle with your faith or doubt God? Did a specific trigger lead you down this path or did your struggle build? What helped bring you back to God, or are you still struggling with your faith?

2. Have you walked with others in their own difficult journeys—infertility or otherwise—when they've had a crisis of faith? Did the experience have an impact on your own faith or how you're handling this cross of infertility right now?

3. To practice imaginative prayer, reflect on John 20:19-29. Be in the scene. You're Thomas—touch Jesus' wounds. Focus on verse 27, when Jesus says, "...do not be unbelieving, but believe." Let Jesus touch your heart, and listen. What's the Lord telling you about doubts you're experiencing?

Week 5: Prayers Seeking Freedom from Waves of Despising God

DAY 30

From the sin of self-pity when I ask, "Why me?" deliver me, Lord...

Everybody experiences pain. The band R.E.M. said it best in their 1992 hit song, "Everybody Hurts".

When experiencing a pain as intense as the pain infertility causes, it's difficult to imagine that anyone else could possibly be hurting as much as you are. For the first few years I struggled to conceive, the emotions I experienced forced me inward. I was so focused on "self"—my pain, my anger, my loss—that I became blind to the struggles of my friends, family and the world at large. My life was so devoid of the love and happiness I believe I deserved that I felt entitled to take from others to fill the void.

I'm ashamed to admit to comparing my pain from suffering from infertility with what I perceived to be a lack of suffering of a loved one. It felt so unfair that I was experiencing such a heavy cross while my loved ones seemed to have little suffering, if at all. One friend, in particular, seemingly had all her heart desired and even whatever she prayed for. Not only was I envious and angry, but in my own self-pity, I wanted her to be pushed into the deep well of suffering as well. In reality, her life wasn't void of suffering, but, even if it was, resenting what I perceived as her life of ease didn't help me any. Wanting reassurance that others were going through their own painful experiences was the enemy whispering lies to me, filling my life with even more negative feelings and leaving little room for peace or joy.

But how do we not wallow in self-pity when Jane Doe's greatest obvious struggle is keeping up with her yard, or whatever seemingly insignificant problem she's complained about?

I believe the answer is to only focus on the transformation occurring inside you. Even Jesus experienced pain. While there were moments when He prayed that the cup pass from Him, He kept on going with courage. He didn't go back and talk for hours on end with His friends, who were supposed to be staying watch for Him, about how incredibly difficult His cross would be. Jesus didn't let His cross keep him from ministering to those around Him. In fact, it propelled Him, and His suffering ultimately gave the entire world the possibility of transformation needed for their salvation.

The cross of infertility has the same power. Infertility has forced me to rely more deeply on God. It has brought a deeper intimacy to my marriage. I'm being transformed, and in a beautiful way.

> *Jesus didn't let His cross keep him from ministering to those around Him.*

I'm a better version of myself now than before I realized I suffered from infertility. I'm stronger and more resilient, authentic and compassionate. Yes, my friend only has her yard to worry about, but I've been transformed!

Reflections

1. Can you recall a time when your emotions regarding your struggle with infertility felt all-consuming? Did that experience throw you into self-pity? If not, how did you handle it? If you have struggled with self-pity, how have you climbed out of those moments?

2. Have you caught yourself comparing someone else's struggles—or lack thereof—to your own suffering? Did you share these thoughts with another person, potentially leading them to think poorly of that person or disregard their suffering? Or did you confront the person with these comparisons? Consider if you need to repair any broken relationships.

3. One way to handle self-pity is to learn from Jesus allowing His cup of suffering to propel Him forward to serve and love others. Think of someone who's shared their struggles with you. How might you love and serve them, even ease their suffering when possible?

4. Ask God to reveal how you've been transformed by the cross of infertility. What further areas of growth and transformation is God asking you to surrender?

Week 5: Prayers Seeking Freedom from Waves of Despising God

DAY 31

From the temptation to believe I'm not woman enough because I'm unable to conceive, deliver me, Lord...

Our culture and Church honor women's bodies as great carriers, bearers and nourishers of new life. How many paintings have you seen of the Madonna pregnant or nursing? Even in secular society, women's bodies are revered as being strong and capable of this precious vocation that no man would ever be able to do. Young children, keenly aware of the sacredness of carrying life, imitate being pregnant and nursing baby dolls in their play.

It's understood that most women, save those in religious life or who are called to a life of chastity in a similar way, will someday go through pregnancy and childbirth, nurse an infant and become mothers. This norm represents the respected role of women in every corner of the earth since the beginning of time.

Discovering that my body isn't capable of co-creating new life with my husband and God has often left me feeling "less than," as if, somehow, the dysfunction of my reproductive system has removed a sacred piece of my femininity. I've often felt robbed of what our culture and the Church hold so precious as to what being a woman means.

On one particular day in my infertility journey, these feelings overcame me. I can't recall what brought them on so strongly, but I felt ashamed as a woman and a wife that I couldn't do this very basic function. I felt broken and guilty that I couldn't "give" my husband a child. I heard whispering of deceitful accusations, "If I can't conceive and carry life within me, what does that mean about me as a woman? The fullness of femininity is found in

> *If I can't conceive and carry life within me, what does that mean about me as a woman?*

a mother with child, and I will never have that."

Praise God for placing dear faith-filled friends in my life for moments such as these. I was soon on the phone with a dear priest friend, begging for answers to the nagging questions filling me with doubt and shame. He was the voice of God to me in that moment. This very busy priest, who no doubt had a mountain of work to tend to, offered me his full attention and spoke love to me.

"You are not broken, Jen," he said. "God does not see you as broken. He made you just the way you are, as His masterpiece."

His words were later reaffirmed on a women's retreat. Still fighting these same feelings, I began journaling during a time of reflection. I wrote, "God made me perfectly in His image. He designed every part of me with loving attention. No part of me was overlooked or forgotten."

Reading these words of divinely inspired affirmation, from both my priest friend and my own reflection, still brings me to tears today and reassures me of my femininity and wholeness.

St. John Paul II wrote in his letter to women, "Thank you, every woman, for the simple fact of being a woman! Through the insight which is so much a part of your womanhood you enrich the world's understanding and help to make human relations more honest and authentic."[7]

There's more to being a woman than whether she can conceive, carry and bear a child.

Author Karen Doyle, who wrote *"The Genius Project,"* which explored St. John Paul II's teaching on the value and dignity of womanhood, said that some of the qualities that mark the feminine genius include receptivity, sensitivity, generosity and maternity—maternity as having the capacity for motherhood, both physically and spiritually.

Women are natural nurturers, and I nurture those in my life in a way only I can—most importantly, my husband. I nurture my

---

[7] St. John Paul II to Women, June 29, 1995 in *Letter of Pope John Paul II to Women.* www.vatican.va/content/john-paul-ii/en/letters/1995/documents/hf_jp-ii_let_29061995_women.html.

parents as they age and my friends in their times of need. Even without a child, I can use my unique gift as a woman to reach out and care for those around me, increasing my capacity to love.

In an earlier apostolic letter on the vocation and dignity of women, *"Mulieris Dignitatem,"* St. John Paul II wrote, "Therefore the Church gives thanks for each and every woman: for mothers, for sisters, for wives; for women consecrated to God in virginity; for women dedicated to the many human beings who await the gratuitous love of another person; for women who watch over the human persons in the family, which is the fundamental sign of the human community; for women who work professionally, and who at times are burdened by a great social responsibility; for 'perfect' women and for 'weak' women—for all women as they have come forth from the heart of God in all the beauty and richness of their femininity; as they have been embraced by his eternal love; as, together with men, they are pilgrims on this earth, which is the temporal 'homeland' of all people and is transformed sometimes into a 'valley of tears'; as they assume, together with men, a common responsibility for the destiny of humanity according to daily necessities and according to that definitive destiny which the human family has in God himself, in the bosom of the ineffable Trinity."[8]

In those now fleeting moments when I'm tempted to believe that I'm any less of a woman than one able to physically bear new life, I recall how I'm God's masterpiece, "made perfectly in His image, intricately designed with loving attention, no part being overlooked or forgotten." God isn't ashamed of me, and I'm not broken. My husband isn't ashamed of me. I'm not ashamed of me.

If God is asking me to open my heart to see how He is calling me in a unique way to use my gift of my femininity to love and nurture others, I'll courageously look for opportunities to care for anyone He brings into my life. I believe He has a special plan for our feminine gifts, a purpose no other woman could have.

---

8 St. John Paul II, *Mulieris Dignitatem*, apostolic letter, Vatican website, August 15, 1988, *www.vatican.va/content/john-paul-ii/en/apost_letters/1988/documents/hf_jp-ii_apl_19880815_mulieris-dignitatem.html*.

So, for those of us struggling right now, we must push away the lies that we're anything less than whole. The enemy longs to steal our joy—don't let him. Rest in the truth that we were made perfectly in the image and likeness of God, and our very being reflects and honors Him in a way no other woman or human can.

"You formed my inmost being; you knit me in my mother's womb. I praise you, because I am wonderfully made…" (Ps 139:13-14a).

Reflections

1. Do you struggle with the lie that you're not woman enough because you cannot conceive or carry a child? When did you feel this lie taking root in your life, and what makes it worse? Have you allowed others' uncharitable comments that support this lie to harbor in your heart?

2. What are your unique gifts of femininity? How do you show your capacity to care for others? Consider asking your husband and close loved ones how they recognize your unique gifts of femininity, too. They may see something in you that you might not otherwise notice. Make a list of all of these gifts on your phone to reference as needed.

3. What does knowing that you were made in the image and likeness of God mean to you? How does your infertility fit into this knowledge?

4. Consider checking out "The Feminine Genius" podcast, which celebrates women of God and our unique genius. Learn more at *www.femininegeniuspodcast.com*.

Week 5: Prayers Seeking Freedom from Waves of Despising God

DAY 32

From the sin of blasphemy, deliver me, Lord...

When we blaspheme God, we insult or show contempt or lack of reverence for Him. When we find ourselves going through a difficult trial or struggling to understand the purpose of our pain, it's easy, and understandable, to turn on God in this way.

Our hearts truly have beautiful desires, and we so long for these desires to come to fruition. For those of us trying to live a life of faith, we see God as part of this beauty. But as we work in concert with Him to live the life He's called us to, and are thrown a major curve ball and are blindsided, God's often the first victim of our contempt.

Of course, expressing frustration to God, or even anger, isn't a sin. All healthy and loving relationships must have a foundation of honesty. What kind of relationship would we have with our Lord if we couldn't express frustration and confusion? As long as we ultimately put our trust in Him and know that, at the end of the day, He loves us and wants what's best for us, there's no harm in telling Him how we really feel. God wants us to be forthright with Him.

However, once we start getting carried away with our anger and blame, we may be tempted to fall into blasphemy.

During these times of suffering, when our faith is tested, we must be strong in respecting our heavenly Father. God deserves the highest level of reverence possible—He is our maker. We must pray for deliverance from temptation to blaspheme Him and to let our anger overtake us and our relationship with Him.

Our Lord consistently gives us the opportunity to love Him and to find joy in all situations. The trial of infertility is, perhaps, one of the most important times to find that strength to love God, to respect Him and to show Him reverence. Suffering and trials are mysteries to us, but we have to trust in His divine plan. Somehow, our infertility is part of this plan, even if we won't understand it while we're on this side of heaven. Even if we could design our own plan of salvation, we couldn't write a better one than God has already written.

When I find myself moved to the point of frustration where I want to blame God and show disrespect or insult Him and His ways, I try to remember that He loves me and understands the desires of my heart, and that He will carry me through my pain. I'm honest with Him and scream and cry, but I always finish by opening myself up to receive His grace and His loving arms around me.

Reflections

1. Have you had situations during your struggle with infertility when you have succumbed to the temptation to blaspheme God, to show disrespect for Him or to insult Him?

2. How have you tried to handle your anger toward God during this or other trials?

3. Reflect on Psalms 77:2-11. Can you relate to the anguish of Israel at God's silence when its very existence was at stake? During times when you feel anger or negative emotion bubbling up, consider praying or meditating on this Scripture. Be quiet with the passage and allow God to speak to your heart and respond. Be still with your feelings and your prayer and see what God reveals about you and your relationship with Him.

Week 5: Prayers Seeking Freedom from Waves of Despising God

DAY 33

From the sin of ingratitude, deliver me, Lord...

Ingratitude is a sin against God's love because it fails or refuses to acknowledge divine charity.

Slipping into the attitude of ingratitude is easy when suffering from infertility. Despite having so many beautiful blessings, we don't have what we desire most.

During my struggle with infertility, I was reminded to be grateful for the season of marriage in which my husband and I found ourselves. We often get so caught up in looking ahead that we forget to recognize the joy of our current life.

While we long to be parents and have small children running around the house, blessings can be found in not yet having children. We're blessed with time to focus on our marriage, grow in our vocations as husband and wife, and work on virtues with which we may struggle. We're able to have a regular date night every week—not many families with small children can say the same. We're able to plan vacations on short notice (and my husband and I have).

I know many of us who struggle with infertility often roll our eyes when well-meaning loved ones allude to these blessings. We get frustrated and assume they think being able to do things other families can't somehow alleviates the pain of our infertility struggles. I also know that any one of us would forsake the ease of these blessings if it meant that we'd be blessed with conception. But before we cast aside comments like these, we should stop and think about what they're saying and embrace the truth of it.

Who knows what God is preparing us for? Perhaps we'll need the virtues we've gained during this time of childlessness for another struggle down the road. Or maybe someday, when we

> *Who knows what God is preparing us for?*

do have children, these virtues we've perfected will come in handy when we're ministering to them in their own lives with their own struggles.

While I don't want to imply that we're childless right now because God has more lessons for us to learn before we're allowed to be parents, we should remember that life has its ups and downs. Just as life won't always be as hard as where we find ourselves right now, it won't always be peachy, either.

We travel our journey toward heaven one step at a time, learning as we go so we can help others further down the path. We have the opportunity to not let this struggle be in vain.

Let's try to remember to be grateful for the blessings we clearly have today. From time to time, let's cast aside our worry and doubt and recognize these blessings for what they truly are, and thank God for them.

Reflections

1. Have you ever thought about ingratitude as a sin? Why do you think God wants us to recognize the blessings—small and large—we've been given?

2. Reflect on Philippians 4:6: "Have no anxiety at all, but in everything, by prayer and petition, with thanksgiving, make your requests known to God." Notice how St. Paul says we should approach God in prayer with thanksgiving—in other words, with grateful hearts. He instructs us to recall all our Lord has done for us, how much He loves us, how much we don't deserve the love that He gives to us anyway. Then reflect on what St. Paul shares in the next verse: "Then the peace of God that surpasses all understanding will guard your hearts and minds in Christ Jesus." How much of God's peace do you think comes from having a grateful heart? Could you find greater peace if you were able to more easily recognize and praise God for His goodness?

3. My journal of thanksgiving has brought such comfort over the years. Have you ever kept a gratitude journal? Describe your experience. If you have never kept one before, consider starting one. Every day, write down something for which you're grateful. It can be as obvious as the roof over your head or something that makes your heart swell, like having a thoughtful spouse who made you feel extra special that day. Over time, see if intentionally calling to mind your many blessings shifts your heart to gratitude. You might be able to recall those blessings more easily during times of suffering and find peace in that moment. There's nothing to lose in trying!

Week 5: Prayers Seeking Freedom from Waves of Despising God

DAY 34

From the paralysis generated by stunted dreams and hopes too small, deliver me, Lord...

I once read a spiritual reflection theorizing that we often find ourselves, perhaps unknowingly, "paralyzed by stunted dreams and hopes too small." The idea has remained with me, even though I've never been able to find the original reflection again.

What I find enlightening is how this idea relates to those of us suffering from infertility. I sometimes find myself stuck on conceiving instead of being fully open to the rich blessing of children however God wants to bestow them upon me. Does being so focused on persuading God of what we think is best cause us to miss the beauty of the immense possibilities He has laid out before us? Are we so blinded by our own desires that we miss out on bigger and more beautiful opportunities, like adoption, spiritual parenting or using our cross of infertility to help others?

God's ways aren't our ways, and we need to trust that He has our best interests at heart. We're not forgotten. Deep down in our hearts, I believe many of us realize that. Our heavenly Father knows how we long to parent His children. All we can do is offer up our prayers and petitions and leave them in His hands. Life doesn't come without our Lord's intervention. There's no such thing as an accidental pregnancy, when God was distracted or didn't realize what He was or wasn't doing.

We must have high hopes for God's plans for our families. Just because our family building isn't turning out as we'd originally intended doesn't mean it's not how God originally intended—with even greater possibilities than we can imagine. He's gently urging us to be open to His will and follow Him where He leads us, with a joyful heart.

God created each of us for a specific purpose—several purposes, probably. Our very existence is meant to glorify our Lord, and we must be open to the opportunities He's given us to achieve that goal.

I have to remind myself to trust that His plan will bring me the most complete joy. If we're kicking and screaming about the path we're on, we'll miss the beauty of it. And the beauty isn't just there, it's breathtaking once you take a minute to notice it.

Together, let's have immense hope and free ourselves by dreaming big. May we never be paralyzed by stunted dreams and hopes too small.

Reflections

1. What does this idea of "being paralyzed by stunted dreams and hopes too small" mean to you? How does it relate to your struggle with infertility?

2. In his letter to the Ephesians, St. Paul touches upon the belief that God accomplishes more than we could ever dream: "Now to him who is able to accomplish far more than all we ask or imagine, by the power at work within us, to him be glory in the church and in Christ Jesus to all generations, forever and ever. Amen" (Eph 3:20-21). Similarly, in his Gospel, St. Matthew quotes Jesus speaking to His disciples: "Amen, I say to you, if you have faith the size of a mustard seed, you will say to this mountain, 'Move from here to there,' and it will move. Nothing will be impossible for you'" (Mt 17:20). Our Lord longs to move within our lives, to bless us in ways we can't imagine. Do you believe this? How do you see this as true in your life? Does it offer you hope in your family building journey?

3. Think about, then write down, your hopes and dreams for building your family, either simply stated or descriptively and elaborately detailed. Take these to prayer and present them, as written, to God. Ask Him to receive these hopes and dreams, do with them what He wills and open your eyes and heart to the possibilities He has for you—to help you dream big and recognize the beauty and opportunities He is giving you to accomplish His plan for your salvation. Rest with it during prayerful meditation or silence and see how He responds to you. You may not receive an answer at that moment but keep your eyes open to be able to recognize His response when He gives it. Consider asking your spouse to do this activity with you and share your hopes and dreams with one another.

Week 5: Prayers Seeking Freedom from Waves of Despising God

DAY 35

From the lack of trust that You love me and that I'm worthy, deliver me, Lord...

"I am special. I am worthy. I am beloved and beheld as precious. I am needed. I have a sacred and unique calling that only I have been chosen to do, with the help of God."

This is another passage from that reflection I wrote on my women's retreat. I'd been trying to hush the lies the enemy had been whispering into my heart—that I wasn't good enough, that I didn't deserve to conceive and bear a child, that God didn't love me enough, that I was being punished for a past wrong or sin. In our heads, we know God loves us, but trying to convince our hearts is a whole 'nother feat.

The prayers in this book so far have asked God for freedom from the temptations that accompany the oftentimes painful journey of infertility. But today's prayer focuses on encouragement—encouragement to hold a steadfast faith, to find the strength to keep moving and to maintain hope in God's plan. Most importantly, it's about trusting that we are loved and worthy!

My crisis of faith usually isn't about if God is truly there but, more often, if God is truly there for ME! My difficulty isn't in believing that God loves the world, but that God loves ME!

Some of us battle the temptation to believe that we need to earn God's love by being an even better person or by growing further in holiness. Maybe then He'll bless us with the gift of a child. Many of us feel that we just haven't yet proven to God that we'll be a good mother.

On the contrary, we can never earn God's love. "We love because he first loved us" (1 Jn 4:19). God freely gives us His love.

It's a gift. There's also nothing we could ever do to lose God's love. It's unconditional.

St. Paul asks, "What will separate us from the love of Christ? Will anguish, or distress, or persecution, or famine, or nakedness, or peril, or the sword?…For I am convinced that neither death, nor life, nor angels, nor principalities, nor present things, nor future things, nor powers, nor height, nor depth, nor any other creature will be able to separate us from the love of God in Christ Jesus our Lord" (Rom 8:35, 38-39).

Does God's unconditional love mean that He wants to give us everything we might ever dream to ask for? Not at all! Much of the time, we don't understand or know what we truly want for our own good anyway.

Trusting in God can be difficult when life has already detoured so profoundly from what we imagined would bring us the greatest amount of happiness. While experiencing this intensity in suffering, opening ourselves to completely surrender to God can't happen immediately but will, instead, have to occur over our lifetime. No quick fix will generate comfort in being wholly vulnerable to God, but we must start ourselves along this path. There's no better person to follow than St. Maria Faustina Kowalska.

St. Faustina's entire message centers on Jesus' mercy being poured out for us during times of need. Her vision of Jesus, as depicted by Eugeniusz Kazimirowski, always carries the words, "Jesus, I trust in You." In one of her many conversations with Jesus, He told her: "My child, life on earth is a struggle indeed; a great struggle for My kingdom. But fear not, because you are not alone. I am always supporting you, so lean on Me as you struggle, fearing nothing. Take the vessel of trust and draw from the fountain of life—for yourself, but also for other souls, especially such as are distrustful of My goodness."[9]

Let this last reflection focus on attempting to gain this trust

---

9 St. Maria Faustina Kowalska, *Diary, Divine Mercy in My Soul* (Kraków: Misericordia Publications of the Congregation of the Sisters of Our Lady of Mercy, 2019), No. 1488.

in God's love for us as we recite St. Faustina's Chaplet of Divine Mercy using our favorite rosary beads. Jesus, I trust in You!

ON THE CROSS

Make the sign of the cross: In the name of the Father, and of the Son, and of the Holy Spirit. Amen.

ON THE FIRST LARGE BEAD

St. Faustina's Prayer for Sinners: O Jesus, eternal Truth, our Life, I call upon You and I beg Your mercy for poor sinners. O sweetest Heart of my Lord, full of pity and unfathomable mercy, I plead with You for poor sinners. O Most Sacred Heart, Fount of Mercy from which gush forth rays of inconceivable graces upon the entire human race, I beg of You light for poor sinners. O Jesus, be mindful of Your own bitter Passion and do not permit the loss of souls redeemed at so dear a price of Your most precious Blood. O Jesus, when I consider the great price of Your Blood, I rejoice at its immensity, for one drop alone would have been enough for the salvation of all sinners. Although sin is an abyss of wickedness and ingratitude, the price paid for us can never be equaled. Therefore, let every soul trust in the Passion of the Lord, and place its hope in His mercy. God will not deny His mercy to anyone. Heaven and earth may change, but God's mercy will never be exhausted. Oh, what immense joy burns in my heart when I contemplate Your incomprehensible goodness, O Jesus! I desire to bring all sinners to Your feet that they may glorify Your mercy throughout endless ages (*Diary of Saint Maria Faustina Kowalska*, 72).[10]

You expired, Jesus, but the source of life gushed forth for souls, and the ocean of mercy opened up for the whole world.

---

10 Marian Fathers of the Immaculate Conception of the Blessed Virgin Mary, "How to Recite the Chaplet." *The Divine Mercy*. September 26, 2022. *www.thedivinemercy.org/message/devotions/pray-the-chaplet*

O Fount of Life, unfathomable Divine Mercy, envelop the whole world and empty Yourself out upon us.

(Repeat three times)

O Blood and Water, which gushed forth from the Heart of Jesus as a fount of mercy for us, I trust in You!

ON THE FIRST SMALL BEAD

Our Father: Our Father, Who art in heaven, hallowed be Thy name; Thy Kingdom come; Thy will be done on earth as it is in heaven. Give us this day our daily bread; and forgive us our trespasses as we forgive those who trespass against us; and lead us not into temptation, but deliver us from evil, Amen.

ON THE SECOND SMALL BEAD

Hail Mary: Hail Mary, full of grace. The Lord is with thee. Blessed art thou amongst women, and blessed is the fruit of thy womb, Jesus. Holy Mary, Mother of God, pray for us sinners, now and at the hour of our death, Amen.

ON THE THIRD SMALL BEAD

The Apostles' Creed: I believe in God, the Father almighty, Creator of heaven and earth, and in Jesus Christ, His only Son, our Lord, who was conceived by the Holy Spirit, born of the Virgin Mary, suffered under Pontius Pilate, was crucified, died and was buried; He descended into hell; on the third day He rose again from the dead; He ascended into heaven, and is seated at the right hand of God the Father almighty; from there He will come to judge the living and the dead. I believe in the Holy Spirit, the holy catholic Church, the communion of saints, the forgiveness of sins, the resurrection of the body, and life everlasting. Amen.

FOR THE BEGINNING OF EACH DECADE

Eternal Father, I offer you the Body and Blood, Soul and Divinity of Your Dearly Beloved Son, Our Lord, Jesus Christ, in atonement for our sins and those of the whole world.

ON THE 10 SMALL BEADS OF EACH DECADE

For the sake of His sorrowful Passion, have mercy on us and on the whole world.

IN CONCLUSION

Holy God *(Repeat three times)*: Holy God, Holy Mighty One, Holy Immortal One, have mercy on us and on the whole world.

CLOSING PRAYER

Eternal God, in whom mercy is endless and the treasury of compassion—inexhaustible, look kindly upon us and increase Your mercy in us, that in difficult moments we might not despair nor become despondent, but with great confidence submit ourselves to Your holy will, which is Love and Mercy itself.

St. Augustine of Hippo said, "You have made us for yourself, O Lord, and our heart is restless until it rests in you." To me, this sounds like the ultimate mission in life—our primary vocation. Finally finding rest in God, and aligning our will with His will for our lives, will bring us deep peace and overwhelming joy, even amidst our suffering and hardships, though it seems contradictory.

After all, you're precious, and you're worthy. You're the one of 99 the shepherd deserts his flock to find when you're lost (Lk 15:4-7). Trust, sister, that your infertility doesn't define you. You're so much more to our Lord than someone with potential to give biological life. You, too, have a sacred and unique calling that only you've been chosen to do, with the help of God. He handpicked you out of all of the women who've ever been or will be, and He knows that what He's called you to will bring you great joy.

Does your calling involve motherhood? Maybe.

Does it involve peace, laughter, love and purpose? Absolutely.

In the end, you will not have been able to choose a better path toward heaven if you'd designed it yourself.

I have a special place in my heart for those who suffer from the cross of infertility, and I pray regularly for hurting couples and families. I know from personal experience how difficult and arduous the infertility journey is. While we all wait to have God's will for our families revealed to us, let us unite in faith and trust that He holds each and every one of us in the palm of His hand and knows us intimately and personally, more than we know ourselves.

Reflections

1. Do you struggle with believing God's love for you or in trusting that He's always with you and cares about the desires of your heart? Have you, even unconsciously, thought you needed to be a good person and perform good deeds for God to love you, or to earn His love?

2. How do you feel when you're reminded of God's incredible and unconditional love for you? In his Gospel, St. Luke retells Jesus saying, "Are not five sparrows sold for two small coins? Yet not one of them has escaped the notice of God. Even the hairs of your head have all been counted. Do not be afraid. You are worth more than many sparrows" (Lk 12:6-7). Can you even know the number of hairs on your own head or the heads of those you hold most dear? There's no way. Yet God knows us so intimately and holds us so precious that He knows even this most intricate detail about us. Reflect on Psalms 139:1-16. God's great love story for us is spelled out very clearly in Scripture; we need only to trust and believe it.

3. Consider the idea that God has chosen you for a special and unique purpose. You're the only person throughout all of time who can play this part in salvation history, and God's inviting you to cooperate with Him. Continue to pray and meditate to reveal this purpose. How can you see your family building journey playing a part in this mission? What can you take from your infertility experience to help build God's Kingdom here on earth?

Closing Week 5 with *Courage*

Lord, as I close this week, I acknowledge the times I have failed to desire to be close to You. My hope in You has faltered, and I've lost my ability to trust. Help me to once again feel like I'm in Your presence. Help me surrender my lack of faith!

Deliver me.

Wherever I've been full of faithlessness, fill me with courage! I know a lack of faith is rooted in fear—fear of never experiencing joy and finding peace, and fear that You've forgotten me. Fear overwhelms me and dictates my decisions and actions. It consumes me, but I no longer want fear to rule my life. I pray that I may receive Your courage and grace. Fill my heart so I may surrender my needs to You and follow You in trust and faith.

Lord, I'm letting go. I know my sufferings are not ceasing today, but I now have courage. I'm full of Your grace and will follow You wherever You lead me. I'll be fruitful wherever You plant me. Jesus, I trust in You! Be near me and bless me.

Amen.

Closing Prayer of Discernment

To close out this journey of reflection, intentionally carve out time this last day for quiet reflective prayer. Find a place where you can be still and won't be bothered, turn off your screens and put away any other distractions. Sit with God and speak to Him in whatever way you're most comfortable. Read slowly through the following prompts, taking time after each one to reflect and listen. (If it helps you, consider writing your thoughts and prayers in a journal.) Based on the *Daily Examen* suggested and written by St. Ignatius of Loyola, these prompts aim to help you reflect on the past month and see where God has moved in your journey.

Start with this opening prayer:
"Help me to be present in this moment, Lord. Give me the grace to be quiet, to be still and to feel Your presence here with me. Breathe Your Holy Spirit into this space and open up my ears to hear what You want to tell me. Remove from my mind any thoughts that would cause distraction and that would lead my thoughts away from You. Thank You for helping me find time to be with You here. Amen."

1. **Give thanksgiving.** What are you grateful for this past month? What blessings do you recognize as having come from God, especially in regard to your family building journey? No matter how big or insignificant they may seem, thank Him for the grace to be able to recognize these blessings as well as those you might not have recognized but know were there.

2. **Review and recognize moments of weakness.** Take an honest look back at the past month and ask the Lord to point out the moments when you failed in big or small ways. Where do you feel drawn to ask for forgiveness? Where in your fertility journey have you given in to

turning your eyes away from God? How might you be able to better handle a similar situation in the future? Do you need to make any changes or apologize to others? Is there anyone you need to forgive to free your heart from anger or resentment?

3. **Pray about the next month.** Let the Lord show you how the month ahead might go. Consider upcoming plans, people you'll likely see and decisions needing to be made. Are there any triggers that may tempt you to sin or struggle? Any baby-related events or doctor's appointments? Any child-centered holidays? Pray for God's presence during the moments you foresee being difficult. How can you prepare yourself to be the best version of yourself and a holy witness of God's love?

4. **Where are you right now in your journey toward parenthood?** Check in with your spouse to pray together about what God is calling you to do this month to build your family. What options do you have? Do you feel ready to continue with treatment next month, or do you need to take a break? Does your spouse?

5. **Where are you right now spiritually?** Do you feel close to God or distant from Him? Are you angry or bitter, or positive and hopeful? Are you finding peace where you're at in your journey toward parenthood, or are you anxious and in need of rest? If you're feeling spiritually healthy—wonderful. But if you're feeling any uneasiness or as though you're stuck, consider speaking to a spiritual director, priest or deacon, or someone whose faith you admire, for help getting back on the path of striving for peace and finding joy in following God's will. And, as always, be open and honest with God about all you've been feeling. If you're angry, tell Him; He can handle it. Verbalizing or writing down what you've been holding

CLOSING PRAYER OF DISCERNMENT

in may be therapeutic and help you process it. Let it out. It's important to continue to develop your relationship with God and communicate with Him, not to ignore Him.

Final Thoughts

Wherever you may find yourself in your family building journey at this time, please know that I am praying for you, along with the entire ministry of Sarah's Hope & Abraham's Promise. The cross of infertility is difficult to bear, especially when you feel alone or like no one understands what you, your marriage and your body are going through. Your emotions can become overwhelming from time to time, so I hope this first in my series of devotionals for women struggling with infertility has helped give your prayer life direction. If a specific day's prayer and reflection especially resonated with you, go back and pray on it—for as many days, weeks or months as you're drawn to it. Keep this devotional handy for rough days, so you can pray through the entire litany or go directly to the lines and reflections that speak to you or what you're struggling with in that moment.

While only God knows how long this journey of continual hoping followed by disappointments may last, may He reveal to you, in His perfect time, His plans for your family. I pray He grant you the strength to bear this suffering well and give you increased hope and trust for what He has in store for you.

If you're interested in learning more about Sarah's Hope & Abraham's Promise and finding a chapter near you, please visit *www.hopeforinfertility.com*. We offer many resources and the opportunity to connect with community for support and encouragement.

Just remember, you're not alone in the boat being rocked about by those stormy waves of grief from infertility. Though it may sometimes feel like a lonely place to find yourself, know that your faith community supports you and is here to offer you prayers and hope. Recognize where you're at and be encouraged that your family building journey, while very difficult at times, has the power to transform you as you're drawn closer to God. May you feel His presence in your life and be comforted in believing that He's holding you in the palm of His hand.

When you're ready, look for the next book in my series of devotionals for women struggling with infertility: "The Rescue." The second volume of "Praying Through Infertility: A litany and devotional for women" supports the next step in our infertility journey. After experiencing the "Stormy Waves of Grief," we, like Peter, begin to have hope for a miracle in our lives, and we gather the courage to step out of our metaphorical boat and take a chance, yet again, to try to conceive. Prayers in "The Rescue" focus on what happens after we step out but then take our eyes off Jesus. We find ourselves sinking, consumed by the negative emotions the evil one uses in his plans to push us under once and for all. It seems hopeless, but "The Rescue" will illuminate Jesus' hand reaching out to you, keeping you afloat. You will be guided through petitions to see this rescue more clearly, to have the courage to take His hand and to receive the fortitude to walk toward your own miracle of healing.

May God richly bless you, and may your heart find rest in Him!

Love, Jen

APPENDIX

Additional Resources

FINDING A DOCTOR

NaProTECHNOLOGY (natural procreative technology) monitors and maintains a woman's reproductive and gynecological health. Its medical and surgical treatments cooperate completely with the reproductive system. In 2004, Thomas W. Hilgers, MD, the director of the Pope Paul VI Institute for the Study of Human Reproduction and the National Center for Women's Health, published the definitive textbook on natural procreative technology, *The Medical and Surgical Practice of NaProTECHNOLOGY.*

Pope Paul VI Institute
6901 Mercy Road
Omaha, Nebraska 68106
(402) 390-6600
WWW.POPEPAULVI.COM

To find a doctor in your area who's trained in NaProTECHNOLOGY, visit the website of FertilityCare Centers of America at *www.fertilitycare.org* and click on "Find a Medical Consultant" under the NaProTechnology drop-down menu.

INFERTILITY, PREGNANCY LOSS AND ADOPTION SUPPORT

A ministry of the Rabboni Institute for Learning & Healing, Sarah's Hope & Abraham's Promise (SHAP) provides spiritual and emotional healing, support and education to couples struggling with infertility or pregnancy loss or who have been touched by adoption. SHAP's vision is to help hurting couples and families find peace, faith and community in their family building journey.

You can bring SHAP programs to your area by:
- Hosting an event, such as a healing retreat, prayer service or Mass
- Purchasing Bible studies, books or study guides to use individually or in a group setting
- Starting a local chapter to host support groups in your parish or area
- Collaborating on a project as part of a ministry with programs that overlap with SHAP

Sarah's Hope & Abraham's Promise
Austin, Texas
(512) 736-7334
WWW.HOPEFORINFERTILITY.COM
shap@teachmehealme.com

Rabboni Institute for Learning & Healing
This full-spectrum healing ministry combines traditional medicine and psychological services with the power of prayer and the sacraments.

Rabboni Institute for Learning & Healing
Austin, Texas
(512) 484-2405
WWW.TEACHMEHEALME.COM
info@teachmehealme.com

The Fruitful Hollow
The Fruitful Hollow is a Catholic resource and community for those who struggle with infertility. Here you will feel heard, find understanding, dive into Church teachings and be inspired by stories of fruitfulness in the wait. They publish weekly blog posts, create monthly resources and host a mentorship ministry.

WWW.THEFRUITFULHOLLOW.COM
thefruitfulhollow@gmail.com

Springs in the Desert

This ministry accompanies those struggling with infertility by offering a place of respite and solidarity where they can know God's love for them and discover His unique call to fruitfulness. Firmly rooted in the anthropology, ethics and spirituality of the Catholic Church and shared experiences of infertility, Springs in the Desert affirms the goodness of marriage, upholds the giftedness of the child and advocates for a broader understanding of what it means to be life-giving. By keeping the focus on Christ, not on conception, this ministry gives witness to His Divine love and mercy and the goodness of His plan for our lives.

HTTPS://SPRINGSINTHEDESERT.ORG

COUNSELING HELP

Being able to talk through your feelings with a therapist or counselor can be extremely helpful. To find a qualified counseling professional with whom you're comfortable sharing, and who is faithful to the magisterium of the Catholic Church, contact your diocese for a list of counselors in your area or visit *CatholicTherapists.com*.

WWW.CATHOLICTHERAPISTS.COM
Melbourne, Florida
catholictherapists.com/about/contact

BOOKS

Be Healed: A Guide to Encountering the Powerful Love of Jesus in Your Life by Dr. Bob Schuchts

"Be Healed" is a guide to spiritual, emotional and physical healing through the power of the Holy Spirit and the sacraments. This renowned program for spiritual restoration is steeped in Scripture and the wisdom of the Catholic Church. Deeply intimate and vulnerable about his own journey of healing, Catholic therapist and John Paul II Healing Center founder Dr. Bob Schuchts connects with readers by sharing the series of betrayals he endured as a young man and his subsequent seasons of struggle with God and faith. "Be Healed" is based on the program first used in dioceses across the United States to form the hearts and minds of Catholic clergy. Schuchts' trusted process for finding inner peace and healing has expanded to serve the entire body of Christ, helping people recognize their brokenness and find hope in the Risen Christ.

APPENDIX

Facing Infertility: A Catholic Approach by Jean Dimech-Juchniewicz

Couples experiencing infertility find themselves in a "desert"—lost and abandoned, hungering and thirsting, praying and waiting for a child. Navigating through the desert of infertility is an especially painful experience that can lead to a sense of failure and a feeling of hopelessness, especially Catholic couples who perceive a lack of sufficient infertility resources to help them. As a Catholic woman who personally struggled with infertility and who heard a woman's prayer group discussion on the scarcity of such resources, Jean Dimech-Juchniewicz understood this predicament perfectly and was inspired to fill this void with "Facing Infertility: A Catholic Appproach." Blending Catholic teaching with the best medical science has to offer, this spiritual companion gives readers the direction, nourishment and faith to find their way out of the desert and onto a path to healing in a sensitive and gradual manner. The morality or immorality of various infertility treatment options are explained within the context of Church teachings. This resource also delves into the emotional, psychological, medical, biological, cultural and financial aspects to dealing with infertility. Each chapter contains a Scripture passage, a reflection from a Catholic woman who has been struggling with infertility, commentary, discussion questions, tips for friends and family and a prayer from the Book of Psalms.

The Infertility Companion for Catholics by Angelique Ruhi-López and Carmen Santamaría

One in every six U.S. couples experiences infertility, but Catholic couples face additional confusion, worry and frustration as they explore which medical options are available to them. Filling a major void in Catholic resources, "The Infertility Companion for Catholics" describes the Church's teaching on reproductive technologies and provides a rich spiritual perspective on the emotions and faith involved in embracing the cross of infertility. Both authors experienced periods of being unable to conceive, and they walk in solidarity with readers, compassionately coaching them through the challenging landscape of infertility. This book contains a variety of spiritual resources, such as prayers, devotions and the wisdom of the saints, as well as a chapter designed specifically for friends and family members, with tips on how to relate to infertile couples with compassion and sensitivity. The appendices include suggested further reading, reference materials, Catholic documents and Catholic blogs about infertility.

Infertility—Finding God's Peace in the Journey by Lois Flowers

From her own experience, Lois Flowers understands the struggle and anguish her readers go through. She gently points out strategies to help bring true peace and joy in the midst of the disappointment, including making biblically informed decisions about medical treatments to lay the groundwork for future contentment, working out practical ways to deal with family and friends to make reminders of infertility less painful, and praying for God's will, even in the middle of infertility, to bring peace and freedom in all areas of life and a deeper, more authentic experience of God's love and compassion.

Twelve Stripes Deep: How Infertility & Other Suffering Delivered My Greatest Joys by Mary Bruno

This is not your typical infertility journey. It is a love story painted by three dramatic characters—God, suffering and the surprising joy that comes from leaning into both of them. After about 20 years of physical pain and seven years of infertility, Mary's worst fears came true—her doctor recommended a hysterectomy. She began writing a blog series to describe her trek, which, despite the suffering it brought, has delivered her most incredible joys. It begged her for more detail and gave birth to a memoir.

As a Catholic, the implications of infertility are especially troubling when you consider how the call to "be fruitful" is often interpreted. But as St. John Paul II describes in *Mulieris Dignitatem*, "The motherhood of every woman...is not only 'of flesh and blood': it expresses a profound 'listening to the word of the living God' and a readiness to 'safeguard' this Word...(cf. Jn 6:68)." God calls all women to be mothers and to express our originality into the world through our unique talents and the gift of spiritual motherhood. This is a profoundly healing message for women with and without children.

Without Moral Limits: Women, Reproduction and Medical Technology by Debra Evans

Throughout history, women have traditionally passed along their knowledge of womanhood to their daughters, who in turn entrusted their own daughters with these precious secrets. Sadly, this tradition has been lost. But at what cost? In this powerful book, Debra Evans eloquently and clearly presents what thousands of pages of research has documented: women's healthcare is in crisis. Evans details how medical "experts" have taken the place of mothers and grandmothers, how the womb has been rendered optional for procreation now that new techniques allow life to begin in a petri dish, and how doctors are "liberating" women from their biological, God-designed destiny and are disregarding medical and moral norms at the expense of their patients' emotions, finances and bodies. She also shows how, as the traditional domain of women has become the technical domain of doctors, our reproductive competency and dependence on God has increasingly eroded and been sabotaged by our trust in medical professionals and their technology. But Evans also reminds us of a better way, one that understands God's wonderful plan for sexuality and childbearing —and realizes that therein lies the greatest hope for women.

LITANY OF HUMILITY

O Jesus, meek and humble of heart, Hear me.
From the desire of being esteemed, Deliver me, O Jesus.
From the desire of being loved, Deliver me, O Jesus.
From the desire of being extolled, Deliver me, O Jesus.
From the desire of being honored, Deliver me, O Jesus.
From the desire of being praised, Deliver me, O Jesus.
From the desire of being preferred to others, Deliver me, O Jesus.
From the desire of being consulted, Deliver me, O Jesus.
From the desire of being approved, Deliver me, O Jesus.
From the fear of being humiliated, Deliver me, O Jesus.
From the fear of being despised, Deliver me, O Jesus.
From the fear of suffering rebukes, Deliver me, O Jesus.
From the fear of being calumniated, Deliver me, O Jesus.
From the fear of being forgotten, Deliver me, O Jesus.
From the fear of being ridiculed, Deliver me, O Jesus.
From the fear of being wronged, Deliver me, O Jesus.
From the fear of being suspected, Deliver me, O Jesus.
That others may be loved more than I, Jesus, grant me the grace to desire it.
That others may be esteemed more than I, Jesus, grant me the grace to desire it.
That, in the opinion of the world, others may increase and I may decrease, Jesus, grant me the grace to desire it.
That others may be chosen and I set aside, Jesus, grant me the grace to desire it.
That others may be praised and I go unnoticed, Jesus, grant me the grace to desire it.
That others may be preferred to me in everything, Jesus, grant me the grace to desire it.
That others may become holier than I, provided that I may become as holy as I should, Jesus, grant me the grace to desire it.

by Merry Cardinal del Val, secretary of state to St. Pius X from the prayer book for Jesuits, 1963

EXAMINATION OF CONSCIENCE FOR THOSE SUFFERING FROM INFERTILITY

Examining your conscience regularly will keep your relationship with God open and sincere in your pursuit of holiness. It allows God to bring light to something you may need to work on or seek reconciliation for as you continue to grow in faith as a daughter of God.

There are many examinations of conscience. The following was derived from the litany prayer upon which this devotional is based. You can use it alone or along with an additional examination of conscience as you feel the Spirit move you.

Despair:

In my experience with infertility, have I given in to despair, especially on the first day of a new cycle?

Have I despaired against hope and failed to believe that God has my best interest in mind, or lost hope in God turning even this heartache into something good?

Have I given in to weariness?

Have I believed the cross of infertility to be more than I can bear?

Have I believed the lie that I somehow deserve this cross of infertility?

Have I failed to look for and recognize beauty in my life?

Have I doubted I will ever feel joy again until I am able to conceive and bear a child?

Selfishness:

Have I been selfish in my journey with infertility?

Have I tried to grasp, control and make demands of God, myself or others?

Have I dwelled on my hurt feelings when my loved ones fail to ask about my infertility struggle or when I'm not invited to activities of children in my life?

Have I made others' pregnancies more about myself and my not being pregnant rather than celebrating the gift of new life they've been given?

Have I displayed poor body language around others who've been blessed with children?

Have I dismissed the struggles of others as trivial compared to my own?

Envy:

Have I given in to the spirit of envy in my experience with infertility?

Have I allowed resentment to build toward others who don't struggle with infertility?

Have I scoffed at those who speak of timing their pregnancies at their convenience?

Have I discouraged those who speak of their ideal plan to grow their family?

Have I reacted poorly or uncharitably when someone announced a pregnancy?

Have I allowed frustration to influence my behavior toward women who bring up their past pregnancies or dwell on stories about their children?

Have I been insensitive and flaunted the freedom my child-free life offers in front of others who have children?

Anger:

Have I given in to the spirit of anger in my experience with infertility?

Have I obsessed over my struggles with infertility?

Have I complained excessively?

Have I been impatient?

Have I been quick to take offense?

Have I been rash when pursuing solutions to my infertility without pausing to consider the consequences of each option?

Have I been quick to judge the decisions of others about the way they pursue, or choose not to pursue, building their family?

Faithlessness:

Have I given in to the spirit of faithlessness in my experience with infertility?

Have I given in to self-pity?

Have I failed to believe that my gifts of femininity make me the masterpiece God designed me to be, just the way I am? Have I thought that God overlooked some part of me or that I am broken as a woman? Have I given in to the lie that I'm not woman enough if I'm unable to conceive and bear children?

Have I been blasphemous?

Have I been ungrateful for the many gifts God has given me?

Have I been paralyzed by stunted dreams and hopes too small?

Have I failed to trust that God loves me and that I am worthy?

Carelessness:

In my experience with infertility, have I given in to overindulgence to numb my pain, especially on the first day of a new cycle?

Have I persevered in offering up all sorrows?

Have I tried to remain hopeful, find God's peace and look for joy on the first day of a new cycle?

Have I tried to be positive and committed to restoring my body to its normal menstrual cycle pattern and my reproductive system to full health through natural procreative technology as well as seeking God's will for my family?

Have I been patient in my suffering and persevered in faith?

Self-Interest:

Have I allowed feelings of chaos, confusion and distrust in God to overwhelm me when infertility treatments haven't resulted in conception?

Have I sought to place blame or criticism on myself or others instead of seeking acceptance and increasing in hope?

Have I failed to acknowledge the righteousness of God and my great need for Him in all things?

Have I allowed feelings of shame to drive me away from being in community and relationship with others?

Have I made a sincere effort to rejoice with others when hearing pregnancy announcements?

Have I sought the peace of God when hearing pregnancy announcements?

Have I tried to endure my suffering with a display of patience when hearing pregnancy announcements?

Have I tried to be selfless and place the good of others above my own when hearing pregnancy announcements?

Have I tried to remain faithful to God's plan for my family when hearing pregnancy announcements?

Have I shown politeness and restraint of any negativity when hearing pregnancy announcements?

Have I held onto any resentments and failed to forgive those who have wounded me through this infertility struggle?

In my experience with infertility, have I been compassionate, loving and kind to others?

Have I tried to put myself in others' shoes and see things from their perspective?

Awareness of God's Goodness:

Have I been able to praise God for the gifts of life He has granted to our loved ones?

Have I tried to increase in holiness? Have I been intentional about asking for the grace to be a holy spouse, in becoming the wife God has called me to be to my husband?

Have I allowed the suffering from my cross of infertility to strengthen my marriage and draw me closer to my spouse and to God?

Have I embraced God's gift of the cross of infertility?

Have I been intentional about not allowing my infertility to completely remove my focus from other areas of my life that need my time and attention?

Have I remembered to be merciful to myself?

Have I tried to increase in holy indifference, seeking to find peace in aligning my will with God's will for me?

Ignorance:

Have I tried to accept where I am in my fertility journey?

Have I demonstrated faith that God can turn all things, even my infertility, into good?

Am I holding resentment toward my spouse for any aspect of our infertility?

Am I holding resentment toward myself for our infertility?

Am I holding resentment toward God for our infertility?

Have I been stubborn in refusing to address and work through the grief from our infertility, thereby missing the opportunity to receive God's healing?

Have I considered the opportunity that infertility has given me for sanctification in helping me become the saint God's called me to become?

Discernment:

Have my spouse and I been aware of our own health—physically, mentally, spiritually, emotionally and financially—and prayed about taking breaks in actively trying to conceive?

Have my spouse and I been prayerful about knowing if the time should come for us to end all active treatments in trying to conceive?

Have my spouse and I been prayerful in seeking God's will for the future of our family?

Have I taken to heart the words of support and prayers from trusted and faithful loved ones through whom God might have used to convey His will for our family?

Have I been open to exploring our call to using the path of adoption to build our family?

Have I been willing to die to self in my desire for children and be open to truly discerning God's will for our family?

Have I tried to both be open with my spouse about my personal desires for our family building journey as well as be open to hearing and considering my spouse's desires?

Discipleship:

Have I actively sought and recognized the work of the Holy Spirit in my life?

Have I witnessed my faith and love for God by word and example when given the opportunity?

Have I taken the opportunity to use God's gift of the cross of infertility to build His Kingdom here on earth?

Have I been intentional about embracing my call to spiritual motherhood in loving, encouraging, praying for and supporting the children in my life, especially my godchildren?

Have I recognized opportunities to love and serve others?

Have I been open to allowing God's grace to bear fruit in my life through my infertility?

Have I contributed my time, talent and treasure to building God's Kingdom?

Love:

Have I prayed for and supported others struggling to conceive, those who have experienced a pregnancy loss or early infant loss and those who remain childless in their marriage?

Have I been supportive of my spouse during our infertility experience and his struggles and weaknesses?

Have I used any opportunies to increase awareness and reduce the stigma of infertility in my parish and community when it felt necessary?

Have I encouraged in my community respect for the sanctity of life?

Have I prayed for, supported and thanked the people, Church and organizations who minister to me and my spouse as well as other couples struggling with infertility and pregnancy loss as well as those touched by adoption?

Have I intentionally placed my marriage as a priority above all else, under my relationship with God? Do I focus effort on nourishing my marriage and relationship with my spouse outside of our family building efforts?

BOOK REVIEWS

Did you enjoy this book?

Thank you for reading *Praying Through Infertility*! May I make a request?

Will you please take a moment and leave an honest review on Amazon, Goodreads or where you purchased the book? Reviews are the single best way to help others discover the book.

Thanks in advance!

ABOUT THE AUTHOR

Jennifer Crowley, better known as Jen, has more than 15 years of pastoral experience, serving especially adults in their 20s and 30s in need of community and faith support. As a co-founder of Sarah's Hope & Abraham's Promise Ministry with Cari Henry, MD, Jen is grateful to have found her calling to offer spiritual and emotional support to those struggling with infertility or pregnancy loss, as well as support for those touched by adoption. She serves as division director for Sarah's Hope & Abraham's Promise, overseeing and supporting all chapters and activities of the ministry nationwide.

Jen has personally experienced the cross of infertility for more than 10 years and is familiar with the ups and downs the infertility journey can bring. She is passionate about bringing awareness to the family building struggles so many couples go through, and providing connection and community to those who are hurting. She feels blessed to provide validation, comfort and faith encouragement to the women and men who too often suffer in silence.

As a graduate of the School of Journalism from the University of Texas at Austin, Jen worked in magazine journalism and public relations for years before she attended a retreat at her parish and was led to work in full-time ministry. She now uses her unique gifts for ministry to serve the people of God.

A Roman Catholic, she has worked at two Catholic parishes in the Diocese of Austin (Texas). She also founded and led a large and dynamic ministry for young adults in their 20s.

Jen has been the proud wife to a great man, Mark, for over 14 years, and has been blessed through the miracle of adoption to be the mama of five beautiful (and very active) children!

She comes from the South and loves cooking, a glass (or two) of wine and Jesus. Throw in a movie marathon coupled with snuggles with her kiddos or deep conversations with her dearest loved ones, and you couldn't find Jen happier!

Check out Jen's contributions to the "Being Fruitful" blog on the Sarah's Hope & Abraham's Promise website, at *www.hopeforinfertility.com*, and follow Sarah's Hope & Abraham's Promise on Facebook, at **WWW.FACEBOOK.COM/SHAPMINISTRY**.

Find Jen online and sign up to join her mailing list at:

WWW.JENCROWLEY.COM

WWW.FACEBOOK.COM/JENNIFERCROWLEYAUTHOR

hello@jencrowley.com

AN INVITATION

Sarah's Hope & Abraham's Promise offers Bible studies, books and study guides that bring people together to form community and find healing in their family building journey. Whether someone finds themselves suffering through infertility or pregnancy loss, or touched by adoption, our program seeks to bring hurting couples and families peace and community during a time they so often find themselves in dire need of connection and encouragement in their faith.

If you answer yes to any of the following questions, visit our website, at *www.hopeforinfertility.com*, to view our resources and services:

- Do you feel called to bring a healing retreat to your area that will offer a transformational experience for those suffering through infertility or pregnancy loss or who have been touched by adoption?
- Could you use support group meetings near you to help with emotional and spiritual encouragement during your family building journey?
- Are you involved with a ministry or organization with programs overlapping ours and interested in collaborating on a project?
- Do you need someone to talk to who understands the struggles you're facing with infertility, pregnancy loss or adoption?

In whatever way you are looking for support for yourself or someone else in this situation, please know that our prayers are with you. Infertility, pregnancy loss and adoption are, or can be, tough situations to live through. The crisis of faith each path can bring is no joking matter, and we want you to know that we're here for you and that there's a community of support for you! We promise that you're not alone. Most of all, know that God is with you, even through this, even when He doesn't feel near at all. He said it Himself: *"And behold, I am with you always, until the end of the age" (Mt 28:20b).*

God bless you always, and may He increase your faith in Him, no matter the consequences.

www.ingramcontent.com/pod-product-compliance
Lightning Source LLC
Chambersburg PA
CBHW070151100426
42743CB00013B/2880